Time to Get Ready

Time to Get Ready

An Advent, Christmas Reader to Wake Your Soul

MARK A. VILLANO

PARACLETE PRESS

BREWSTER, MASSACHUSETTS

2015 First Printing

Time to Get Ready: An Advent, Christmas Reader to Wake Your Soul

Copyright © 2015 by Mark Villano

ISBN 978-1-61261-559-2

The Paraclete Press name and logo (dove on cross) is a trademark of Paraclete Press, Inc.

Library of Congress Cataloging-in-Publication Date

Villano, Mark A.
  Time to get ready : an Advent, Christmas reader to wake your soul / Mark A. Villano.
    pages cm
  ISBN 978-1-61261-559-2
  1. Advent—Meditations. 2. Christmas—Meditations. 3. Epiphany season—Meditations. I. Title.
  BV40.V55 2015
  242'.33—dc23   2015027047

10 9 8 7 6 5 4 3 2 1

Published by Paraclete Press
Brewster, Massachusetts
www.paracletepress.com
Printed in the United States of America

Contents

With gratitude to

the many preachers, teachers,

and other ministers of the Word

who have enriched my life.

* * * * * * *

Introduction
Seasons of Grace

Advent is the beginning of a "new year," that is, the beginning of a new, holy time of prayer and reflection on the revelation of Christ to humanity. With the assistance of this pattern of living and reflecting on the Christian mystery, we hope to more fully participate in that mystery. We seek to open ourselves to the invitations of grace around us. Just as we are immersed in creation, so we want to be immersed in the Spirit. We want the seasons of our lives to become seasons of grace.

* * * * * * *

Where did Advent come from?

The earliest Christians relied almost entirely on the "Lord's Day," the weekly celebration of the day of the Lord's resurrection, to maintain their identity and nourish their mission. By the end of the second century, though, what we now know as liturgical seasons began to emerge. First came an annual feast of Easter, *Pascha*, known throughout the church by about the third century. In some places, its time was determined by a lunar calendar, and in others, by a solar calendar. In both cases, the feast celebrated not one incident but the whole Christian mystery and its impact on people's lives. Not long after, the period of fifty days from Easter to the feast of Pentecost was observed as a "season" of celebration. The mystery of Resurrection was too big for one day: its Scriptures, stories, and implications needed to be unpacked over time. Easter was seen as the perfect time for initiating new

Christians into the life of the community. For those readying themselves for baptism at Easter, a forty-day period of fasting, penance, and more intense instruction developed. The whole community joined them in this spiritual preparation, and thus was born what we know as the Lenten fast, leading to a fuller experience of Easter renewal and feasting.

It was in the fourth century when Christians began celebrating the birth of Jesus. Christmas, like Easter, was more than an observance of a particular event. It was the feast of the Incarnation, of God's self-emptying love and embrace of humanity. Both Eastern and Western Christians eventually settled on December 25 as the feast of the Nativity. And just as with the Paschal feast, a pattern of extension and preparation developed. Christmas expanded into the Christmas season, a period of celebration culminating in feasts of Epiphany, or "manifestations" of Christ: the visit of the Magi, the Baptism of the Lord. A period of preparation for Christmas also developed: the four weeks of Advent.

Advent (from the Latin for "coming") is replete with readings, themes, symbols, and traditions. Advent is a time of expectation and hope. Throughout this holy season we move from hope in Christ's coming in the fullness of time, to joyful anticipation of the Christ child's birth. The goal of the season is to make us more ready to receive the message of Christmas and to engage its meaning in our lives.

● ● ● ●

Everyone can benefit from considering these ancient patterns and seasons of prayer. In a culture where the "holiday season" has been reduced to commercial excess, social obligation, or bland sentimentality, what would it mean to "take back" Advent as a time when spiritual groundwork was paramount? What would it mean to conceive of Christmas as the beginning, rather than end, of a celebratory season — a season meant to open you to a new awareness of God at work in your life?

Consider this book a daily "retreat," a time when you can let go of the activity and noise of your life and simply listen. It is meant to be a companion for personal prayer.

Go to a comfortable place. Light a candle. Pray as you normally would. Then read a reflection. Listen. Pray.

Advent begins four Sundays before Christmas. You can begin these reflections on that first Sunday.

And may we always welcome the light and peace of our merciful God!

By the tender mercy of our God,
   the dawn from on high will break upon us,
to give light to those who sit in darkness and in the
      shadow of death,
   to guide our feet into the way of peace. (Luke 1:78–79)

Time to Get Ready

First Week

Advent
Waiting

"Once upon a time there was . . . ," and then everybody leans forward a little and starts to listen.

We want to know what is coming next. There was a young woman named Mary, and an angel came to her from God, and what did he say? And what did she say? And then how did it all turn out in the end?

The story Christianity tells is one that can be so simply told that we can get the whole thing really on a very small Christmas card or into two crossed pieces of wood. Yet in another sense it is so vast and complex that the whole Bible can only hint at it, a story beyond time altogether.

Yet it is also in time, the story of the love between God and humanity. There is a time when it begins, and therefore there is a time before it begins, when it is coming but not yet here, and this is the time Mary was in when Gabriel came to her. It is Advent: the time just before the adventure begins, when everybody is leaning forward to hear what will happen even though they already know what will happen and what will not happen, when they listen hard for meaning, their meaning, and begin to hear, only faintly at first, the beating of unseen wings.

—FREDERICK BUECHNER

One
Telling Time

Besides this, you know what time it is, how it is now the moment for you to wake from sleep. For salvation is nearer to us now than when we became believers; the night is far gone, the day is near. Let us then lay aside the works of darkness and put on the armor of light. (Romans 13:11-12)

· · · · · · ·

Do you remember learning how to tell time? Leaning what the big hand meant and what the little hand meant? You learned all about "half past," "quarter till," "quarter past."

When I was in kindergarten, we had a big clock with a happy face on it. We would go up to the "happy clock" and the teacher would say, "Show me 2:30!" And we could move the hands around till we found 2:30. I've wondered if kindergarteners today take similar tests with happy digital displays!

Advent comes every year and asks: Do you know what time it is? Have you really learned how to tell time? But Advent time isn't the time we're used to, the time we learned to tell in kindergarten. It's not measured in minutes or seconds, or by dates on a calendar. It's not about counting the days till Christmas. There's a different kind of time we have to learn to tell.

St. Paul in his letter to the Romans says, "You know what time it is." There are different words in the Greek language for *time*. One word is *chronos*. It represents the span of time. That's the time we're used to dealing with: the minutes, days, and hours. We see that time in the dates of our calendar. As soon as we

get up in the morning, it confronts us. It flashes out from the
alarm clock to the coffeemaker. We know all about *chronos*. It's
our time.

But St. Paul uses a different word. He uses *kairos*. This is a different kind, a different quality of time. It refers to a crucial point
in time. *Kairos* is God's time. It's God breaking into our time. It's
not a date on the calendar. It's an event in our lives. It's decisive,
a moment of truth.

> For as the days of Noah were, so will be the coming of
> the Son of Man. For as in those days before the flood
> they were eating and drinking, marrying and giving
> in marriage, until the day Noah entered the ark, and
> they knew nothing until the flood came and swept
> them all away, so too will be the coming of the Son of
> Man. Then two will be in the field; one will be taken
> and one will be left. Two women will be grinding meal
> together; one will be taken and one will be left. Keep
> awake therefore, for you do not know on what day
> your Lord is coming. But understand this: if the owner of
> the house had known in what part of the night the thief
> was coming, he would have stayed awake and would
> not have let his house be broken into. Therefore you
> also must be ready, for the Son of Man is coming at an
> unexpected hour. (Matthew 24:37–44)

Some people never learn to tell this kind of time. They never
really catch on to its significance. As Jesus put it, two people are
working, going about their lives. One is taken, the other is left.
In a world of *chronos*, one never knows who is catching on to the
kairos. Who is really catching on to the deeper possibilities in
life? Who are the ones seizing those moments of truth?

We go on and on, so caught up in *chronos*. We're preoccupied with time that's past and time that's not yet here. *Kairos* is always in the present. I received a Christmas card once that read: "Be present to the present of the present." In other words, be available to the gift of the present moment. Simply and gently being in the present is beginning to grasp *kairos*.

Advent comes each year and says: "This is the time!" Can you recognize it? *Kairos* is here. This is the hour of salvation. This is the time "for you to wake from sleep." Wake up to the here and now. Wake up and see how God is moving in your life. Wake up and learn to tell *kairos* time.

Albert Schweitzer, the great musician, medical doctor, philosopher, and theologian, gave up a flourishing career in Europe to open a clinic in a jungle in central Africa. His hospital is still there. He did that because people needed it and he wanted to do it. There is a famous photograph by W. Eugene Smith: a close-up of his hands writing a letter. In a place where supplies were short, he used anything to write on — envelopes, scraps of paper — anything to stay in contact with people.

In one collection of his writings titled *Reverence for Life*, we find these words: "You know of the disease in Central Africa called sleeping sickness. First its victims get slightly tired, then the disease gradually intensifies until the afflicted person lies asleep all the time and finally dies from exhaustion....There also exists a sleeping sickness of the soul. Its most dangerous aspect is that one is unaware of its coming. That is why you have to be careful. As soon as you notice the slightest sign of indifference, the moment you become aware of the loss of a certain seriousness, of longing, of enthusiasm and zest, take it as a warning. . . ."[1]

Do we ever feel like we're sleepwalking through life? That we're just going through the motions? Is it just another day at work, at school, at church? Just another Christmas? Are we so caught up in the routines and the preparations of these dates on the calendar that we miss what's most important about this time in our lives? How does our soul try to warn us? Do we see the possibilities that exist now, the new beginnings that can only happen now?

Advent comes and says "wake up" to these new possibilities. Listen to those cries of the soul. Be open to God's saving mercy breaking through. Be open to what it is calling us to do.

Two
See and Listen

For out of Zion shall go forth instruction,
    and the word of the LORD from Jerusalem.
He shall judge between the nations,
    and shall arbitrate for many peoples;
they shall beat their swords into plowshares,
    and their spears into pruning hooks;
nation shall not lift up sword against nation,
    neither shall they learn war any more.
(Isaiah 2:3-4)

• • • • • • •

*C*hronos: Our time, our usual way of ordering and measuring our span of time. *Kairos*: God's time, God's invitation breaking into our time. There are moments in our lives when we sense that invitation. We are being called into a deeper dimension of living.

One way *kairos* can break into our lives is through a vision—a vision for our future, a vision of where we want to be. In *kairos,* we see and embrace that new vision.

We become like Isaiah. He gives us a vision of swords being made into plowshares and spears into pruning hooks. A vision of a world where human energies are not robbed by the threat of war, by jealousies, resentments, greed. Rather, our energies are freed up to help us become more just and generous beings.

What does it mean to have a vision? What does it mean to see in a new way? Remember the old bumper sticker from the 1980s: "Visualize World Peace"? (And then there was the cynical retort: "visualize whirled peas.") A vision is not merely thinking happy thoughts. It is not naive. It does not expect quick, easy results. Vision is a creative capacity that can set us on a new path.

To envision what does not yet exist means using our great gift of imagination. When we visualize, we're on our way. When we embrace the vision, part of us is already there. On a subconscious level it is influencing our decisions and how we live in the world. Embracing a vision of peace in the world, for example, moves us to become more just and peaceful in our own lives, in our own circumstances, in our own families.

I was privileged to be with someone when he embraced a new vision of himself. For the first time, he admitted that drinking was a problem for him, that it was hurting his relationships. It was robbing him of so much life. He wanted to start building a new foundation. He made a decision to take the first steps in that new direction. What a moment of truth, of vision. What a moment of *kairos.*

Kairos can be found in listening, too. It's found in how we listen. The Quaker author Parker Palmer wrote a book on vocation called *Let Your Life Speak*.[2] The Latin root within that word *vocation* is *voce*, "voice." He makes the point that when thinking about our vocations, career paths, or life direction we often spend too much time listening to voices outside ourselves, to what others think we should be doing. We listen to the expectations of others. We listen to the standards and goals that others set. We listen to outside voices instead of to the voice within, the voice of our true selves.

First Week

Whose voice are we listening to? Palmer suggests the first question to ask is not, What should I be doing? but rather, Who am I? What gifts have I been given? What interests me? What is meaningful to me? What do I enjoy? What do I value? You don't even have to ask what the world needs, because the world needs everything.

The Lord who gave us our gifts speaks within. You're not supposed to be Albert Schweitzer. You're not supposed to be Mother Teresa. You're supposed to be you, the one God is calling.

It begins with a voice within. Let it guide you and see what happens.

Yet *chronos* still floods our vision and our hearing and our decision making. *Chronos* keeps demanding our attention. It keeps counting down our remaining hours, minutes, and seconds.

Thank God we don't have a way of measuring how much *chronos* we have left. As Jesus said, "You do not know on what day your Lord is coming." I sat with a friend next to her hospital bed once. She was not much older than I was, and she had tumors everywhere. We were talking about life at her parish church. She said, "I guess I'm going to miss Advent this year." I should've said to her: Advent is right here. It came to you.

Advent calls us to remember how God came to us in the past in Jesus and changed our world, to recognize how Christ comes to us now, and to embrace Christ's vision for our future. Advent invites us to live now, to wake up to the possibilities of this day. It calls us to envision, to listen, and to act in faith as all those little moments of truth come our way.

Advent teaches us to tell time again. It says: be ready for *kairos* to break into your life at any moment. This is the time.

Three
Peeling the Orange

· · · · · · · ·

A spiritual director I know uses an image: "Prayer is like peeling an orange." People don't usually focus on the peeling; instead, our mind is on the orange, the next thing that's coming. The problem is that when you get to the orange, your mind is still racing to the next thing, the next stimulus. We've trained it that way. So when the orange comes, we're thinking about something else. The orange, on some level, goes by unappreciated, untasted, unsavored. The fullness of the present is lost.

Prayer is a kind of awareness, a coming into the present moment and finding God there. It's an awareness that sees God present, here and now.

We talk about Advent as a time of waiting and watching. That means it can also be about savoring the moment. It means not jumping ahead, but appreciating what is before us.

> But do not ignore this one fact, beloved, that with the
> Lord one day is like a thousand years, and a thousand
> years are like one day. The Lord is not slow about
> his promise, as some think of slowness, but is patient
> with you, not wanting any to perish, but all to come to
> repentance. (2 Peter 3:8-9)

First
Week

But waiting can be such a hard thing. We're not good at wait-ing, and we can see how our impatience affects different areas of life.

We hear so often how failing to plan for the long term is a real problem in the business world. A company or corporation wants its money now, or wants to keep its stockholders or employees happy now, and so may sacrifice long-term values that involve patience: production values, managerial values, ethical values. There may be short-term gain, but in the long term this impatience is bad for business.

I went through a phase when I was reading a lot of business books. Just go to a bookstore and look at the business sec-tion. It goes on and on. One message is repeated in thousands of those books: for a company to thrive today, it has to care about *process* as much as results. Process is about the here and now as well as the long term.

An example: I worked in a company once where there was a manager who got a lot of things done, but often at the expense of the people who worked for him. After one particular project, I heard one collaborator say, "I'll never work with that guy again." Eventually, less got done. What's true in business is true in our personal lives, as well. When people tell me they feel impatient with others, I sometimes ask if they feel impatient with themselves, too. The answer is usually yes. When we're not patient with ourselves, when we don't allow ourselves to be imperfect and finite, or don't give ourselves time to learn and grow—it shows in the way we treat others.

Romantic relationships are another place where impatience shows itself. People can rush the process, instead of taking the time to truly know another emotionally, intellectually, spiritually. We rush instead of taking the time to build a foundation, a commitment to another's future. We rush instead of appreciating what exists now and allowing it to grow.

Our impatience extends to Advent, too. Are you ready for Christmas when it comes, or are you feeling fed up by December 26, when the celebrating should really be getting started? When I was a kid, I remember getting an Advent calendar, one with the little doors that you open on each day leading up to Christmas. What a nice way to encourage being "present to the present of the present." For me, though, that was asking way too much. All those doors were open long before Christmas!

> But, in accordance with his promise, we wait for new heavens and a new earth, where righteousness is at home. Therefore, beloved, while you are waiting for these things, strive to be found by him at peace, without spot or blemish. (2 Peter 3:13–14)

The great irony: The more impatient we are, unable to wait, the more unsatisfied we are in the long term. But the more we are able to cultivate patience, the more fulfilled we are in the short term and long term. Each day has its "present." Each day has its vision, its opportunity to serve the Lord. In patience, we come to see that.

We need to peel the orange. We need to feel its texture, take in its color, smell its fragrance, feel the spray sting our fingers. We need to be alive now, to live fully in the present, so that when Christmas comes, we'll really taste it.

Four
Fleeing the Present

· · · · · · ·

A voidance also makes it hard for us to wait, slow down, to savor the present. We have such a capacity to flee.

There may be something about the present we don't like, that we fear. The present may not be all that we wish or want it to be. It may be a painful present. We may try to cover it up, move past it too quickly—and so we don't learn from it.

There are typical strategies for avoiding the present: fleeing into the past or the future.

People will choose to live in the past. They'll live in their memories, positive or negative. We may wallow in myths about the "good old days" or be consumed by resentments and grudges. We refuse to let go of past failures and hurts. We allow our mistakes to define us. We allow the past to decide how we will live or view ourselves today.

Or, people will live in the future. People will live through worry. They'll worry about things that will never happen or things they can't change. That's a way to escape from the present, too. Or, they will choose to put off their lives. At "some other time" we'll settle down, or have time for ourselves, or pray, or enjoy life. Someone once said that one of the devil's most destructive tools is to convince us that we "have time." There is always some other time, some other day.

> We have all become like one who is unclean,
>> and all our righteous deeds are like a filthy cloth.
> We all fade like a leaf,
>> and our iniquities, like the wind, take us away.
> There is no one who calls on your name,
>> or attempts to take hold of you;
> for you have hidden your face from us,
>> and have delivered us into the hand of our iniquity.
> Yet, O LORD, you are our Father;
>> we are the clay, and you are our potter;
>> we are all the work of your hand. (Isaiah 64:6-8)

When the people of Israel were exiled to Babylon, they lost everything that was important to them. When they returned from the exile to their own land, they had high hopes. Then they saw Jerusalem. It was devastated. Their hopes were wiped out. They were on the edge of despair. They didn't know if they could go on, if they could start over. They didn't know if they had the strength. The prophet Isaiah helped them go through that present moment, not to escape it, not to avoid it.

He did this by first giving a voice to their feelings: "Our righteous deeds are like a filthy cloth. We all fade like a leaf!" Then he helped them to remember. Yes, they are finite, they are sinners, they can't do it on their own. But God is their Father, their Redeemer, their Lord. Here and now they feel like a lump of clay. But they are clay in the potter's hands. They need to be molded into something new. They can't avoid that process.

If the present moment is tough, dangerous, or lonely, we don't have to escape or avoid it. We can enter that pain and learn from it. We can let it move us to open ourselves to others, to do new things, to start a new pattern. To live in the present is to take responsibility for the present, to accept responsibility for ourselves and how we live. It's to say: we are finite, we are to blame for much of our own misery, we are only lumps of clay. But we are clay in God's hands. We can let ourselves be forgiven, molded, changed—because we know our Redeemer.

If the present moment is happy, we can enter that, too. Some people will choose to avoid even those happy moments, as a way to protect themselves from having to let go of what doesn't last. But we can enter those times, too. We can appreciate them and allow them to color our lives.

When we live fully in the present, we are not a slave to either the past or the future.

But there is still another reason we may seek to flee the present: boredom. Sometimes the present entails waiting, and much of the waiting we do we think of as boring. We think of waiting in lines at the airport or in a doctor's office: we're looking at our watch . . . forty-five minutes off schedule . . . we pick up another *People* magazine . . . we look for another distraction on our smartphone.

That's not Advent waiting. Advent waiting is not passive. It's active.

Beware, keep alert; for you do not know when the time will come. It is like a man going on a journey, when he leaves home and puts his slaves in charge, each with his work, and commands the doorkeeper to be on the watch. Therefore, keep awake—for you do not know when the master of the house will come, in the evening,

or at midnight, or at cockcrow, or at dawn, or else he
may find you asleep when he comes suddenly. And
what I say to you I say to all: Keep awake.
(Mark 13:33–37)

Jesus tells us again to stay awake. "Keep alert"! That's how
we're supposed to wait. He's saying: As you wait for me, be about
the things I've told you to be about. Love, care for one another.
Be alert to one another's needs. Be peacemakers and reconcilers
and healers. Be ready to pray and rest in my presence. Savor life
and don't put it off—because I am with you here and now.

We sometimes use the term "wake-up call." We usually mean
some kind of close call or crisis. But it doesn't have to be a crisis or
near-death experience. Anything can be a wake-up call. Anything
can call us to be present in a new way, to savor, to find God.

Anything can call us to prayer: a family gathering around a
dinner table, or a sunset, or a good conversation with a friend,
or a call or an e-mail from someone with whom we had lost
contact—or even eating an orange. They are all like the church
bells that once called people in a village to pray.

Advent is one of those wake-up calls, one of those bells ring-
ing. We need to let Advent call us to prayer, to the present.

Five
Where Wisdom Lies

• • • • • • •

At that same hour Jesus rejoiced in the Holy Spirit and
said, "I thank you, Father, Lord of heaven and earth,

because you have hidden these things from the wise
and the intelligent and have revealed them to infants;
yes, Father, for such was your gracious will." . . .
Then turning to the disciples, Jesus said to them
privately, "Blessed are the eyes that see what you see!
For I tell you that many prophets and kings desired to
see what you see, but did not see it, and to hear what
you hear, but did not hear it." (Luke 10:21, 23–24)

In considering the story of Jesus welcoming the children after
the disciples tried to send them away, the theologian Romano
Guardini, in his *Meditations on the Christ*, wrote: "The children must
have loved coming to him, otherwise their mothers never would
have brought them."[3] Children saw something in him, and he
saw something in them. Something he called the kingdom of
God.

We used to know what this kingdom was all about. We see
this knowledge in little kids who go up to each other and start
playing without hesitation. We see it in their unreserved trust.
We see it in how they get excited about the smallest things, or
how they communicate so freely and simply.

Somehow, we forget all about the kingdom. The child is
ridiculed or criticized. He has to learn to survive in a hostile
environment. She builds up defenses and wants to look mature.
It's funny that part of becoming spiritually "mature" involves
getting back in touch with the childlike within us. We carry
within us traces of that kingdom that need to be found and freed
up. It's there in the pain that needs to be recognized; it's in the
simplicity, trust, and self-honesty that is waiting to be embraced.
This is not some kind of regression to an inner childishness.
It's an inner parent who attends and guides. It's an adult who

teaches and loves. It's a childlike energy that knows how to dry tears, get up, and start playing again with new eyes.

> Thus says the LORD,
>   your Redeemer, the Holy One of Israel:
> I am the LORD your God,
>   who teaches you for your own good,
>   who leads you in the way you should go.
> O that you had paid attention to my commandments!
>   Then your prosperity would have been like a river,
>   and your success like the waves of the sea;
> your offspring would have been like the sand,
>   and your descendants like its grains;
> their name would never be cut off
>   or destroyed from before me. (Isaiah 48: 17–19)

Advent liturgies rely greatly on the book of the prophet Isaiah, including those chapters that scholars refer to as Deutero-Isaiah: writings from a disciple of the great prophet who was active toward the end of the Babylonian exile. There is sobering honesty and accountability in this section (chapters 40–55 of the book of Isaiah), as well as promises of redemption and a call to trust. This is not a child's trust; it is the childlike trust of those who have suffered and learned. It is a trust that has been earned. *"I am the LORD, your God, who teaches you for your own good."* The message is this: I'm trying to teach you something, and if you'd follow that teaching, your peace, your prosperity would flow *"like a river."* Trust me.

A line from one of the great theologians of the twentieth century, Karl Rahner, comes to mind: "God's will is our well-being." Sometimes we may be afraid of God's will. We don't know where God will take us. It represents the unknown. We're troubled just thinking about it, as if God doesn't have our best interests in mind.

But everything we know says that God's will is our well-being. We know because God has acted in our history. We know because of everything Jesus said and did. We know because in our Advent waiting we hear it again from within: the echo of God's prophet calling forth trust. Even when we are uncertain, even when we must confront what we'd rather avoid, the words come back: My will is your well-being. Trust me.

> But to what will I compare this generation? It is like children sitting in the marketplaces and calling to one another,
>> "We played the flute for you, and you did not dance; we wailed, and you did not mourn."
> For John came neither eating nor drinking, and they say, "He has a demon"; the Son of Man came eating and drinking, and they say, "Look, a glutton and a drunkard, a friend of tax collectors and sinners!" Yet wisdom is vindicated by her deeds. (Matthew 11:16-19)

Of course, there are other images of childhood that could be evoked. Jesus speaks, too, of children refusing to play. How much of the hurt, greed, and defensiveness that people carry into their lives began in childhood experiences? So much of life's task involves going back and finding again that truth within us, that openness and freedom that is God's gift.

I was in a workplace once where a supervisor told me, "You won't get anything done here until you come out and play the game." He wasn't talking about an office game, the "rules" of how to survive in a cutthroat environment. He was advising me to "come out and play," to be known and get to know the gifts and strengths and goals of the people around me, to collaborate with them and make things happen.

"Wisdom is vindicated by her deeds." In other words, time will tell where wisdom lies. It takes a certain kind of trust to see that. It takes the maturity that allows us to drop those layers of illusion that we've lived with for so long. It takes the wisdom that sees the alluring and trustworthy power of truth: the truth that will come to us at Christmas as a child.

Six
Like a Shepherd

Comfort, O comfort my people,
    says your God.
Speak tenderly to Jerusalem,
    and cry to her
that she has served her term,
    that her penalty is paid,
that she has received from the LORD's hand
    double for all her sins. . . .
See, the Lord GOD comes with might,
    and his arm rules for him;
his reward is with him,
    and his recompense before him.
He will feed his flock like a shepherd;
    he will gather the lambs in his arms,
and carry them in his bosom,
    and gently lead the mother sheep.
(Isaiah 40:1–2, 10–11)

· · · · · · ·

If you haven't attended a performance of Handel's *Messiah* for a while, this is the month to look for one. There is nothing like hearing those first sublime strains of the oratorio, wedded to Isaiah's poetry, to signal the Advent spirit to us: "Comfort ye my people. . . ."

First Week

"Consolation" is a spiritual category that comes to our aid in discerning the movements of God's Spirit in our lives. The Spirit brings us what we need. It offers comfort in the midst of distress and weariness. It delivers a promise of an ultimate homeland, and awakens our will to journey toward it. At the same time, "desolation" is just as rich a spiritual indicator, calling us to wider compassion and deeper trust. The old line about prophets knowing how to "comfort the disturbed and disturb the comfortable" is appropriate. There's something in us that needs to be comforted, and there's something in us that needs to be disturbed.

> And the foreigners who join themselves to the LORD,
>> to minister to him, to love the name of the LORD,
>> and to be his servants,
> all who keep the sabbath, and do not profane it,
>> and hold fast my covenant—
> these I will bring to my holy mountain,
>> and make them joyful in my house of prayer;
> their burnt offerings and their sacrifices
>> will be accepted on my altar;
> for my house shall be called a house of prayer
>> for all peoples. (Isaiah 56:6-7)

A "house of prayer for all peoples" sounds like a pretty comforting image. Yet, is this "comfort" precisely where we need to be disturbed? Don't we tend to define for ourselves who all those people are—the ones that we will invite into the Lord's house? Aren't they the people we are comfortable with already? Isaiah's people had been put through the wringer by "foreigners." Are these the ones he is inviting into God's temple?

Or perhaps this is not a literal house at all. Perhaps its poetic challenge goes beyond shared space or chores. Perhaps the welcome being offered is more about our awareness of God's inclusion and the universality of God's call. The challenge then becomes practical in our call to see no one as a "foreigner." The challenge is in our willingness to listen and understand rather than dismiss and judge. It is seen, not in offering a false hospitality or mere approval, but in the offer of acceptance and love.

> What do you think? If a shepherd has a hundred sheep, and one of them has gone astray, does he not leave the ninety-nine on the mountains and go in search of the one that went astray? And if he finds it, truly I tell you, he rejoices over it more than over the ninety-nine that never went astray. So it is not the will of your Father in heaven that one of these little ones should be lost. (Matthew 18:12-14)

The catacombs were the meeting places and burial sites of the early Christians in Rome. The earliest Christian art on the walls there were depictions of Jesus as the Good Shepherd. Why was that image so important to them? Of all the ways that Jesus could be portrayed, why was that the image that resonated with them most?

When we read the passage above about the shepherd who goes in search of the lost sheep, most likely we think of ourselves as the Lord's fold. Others have strayed. We're the "ninety-nine."

The early Christians may have seen it differently. That "one"—the one who is in trouble—that's us. We're the ones who are lost, in mortal danger, alone. And waiting.

Jesus asks, *"Does he not leave the ninety-nine on the mountains and go in search of the one that went astray?"* and the answer is not so clear. There are plenty who certainly would not put ninety-nine at risk to go after just one. The shepherd Jesus speaks of must have valued that one as much as all the others. That one must have been precious in his eyes.

That understanding is at the heart of our faith: knowing we are that precious in God's sight, that we are the object of that divine love and concern: the love that causes the shepherd to risk everything in search of us. When we come to see how far God will go to save us, when we come to know how God sees us, how much God wants our safety and healing, we can face anything.

Our faith, then, is not as much about our knowing and loving God as it is our awareness that we are known and loved by God. Of course, that represents a lifetime of learning. But such awareness is also the easiest message to hear and absorb. It is a matter of opening ourselves to letting it sink in and saying, "Amen."

Seven
Stars

To whom then will you compare me,
or who is my equal? says the Holy One.
Lift up your eyes on high and see:
Who created these?
He who brings out their host and numbers them,

calling them all by name;
because he is great in strength,

mighty in power,

not one is missing. . . .
Have you not known? Have you not heard?
The LORD is the everlasting God,

the Creator of the ends of the earth.
He does not faint or grow weary;

his understanding is unsearchable.
He gives power to the faint,

and strengthens the powerless.
Even youths will faint and be weary,

and the young will fall exhausted;
but those who wait for the LORD shall renew their strength,

they shall mount up with wings like eagles,
they shall run and not be weary,

they shall walk and not faint. (Isaiah 40:25-26, 28-31)

· · · · · · · ·

As Christians we believe that meaning is discoverable: that by delving into creation and human history we can find the truths and meaning that our Creator and Redeemer wants to reveal to us. That does not mean that we do not also invest the world around us with meaning. Once we know the basic truths of our faith, we see them reflected all around us. All things begin to announce the Good News; every creature starts to sing. Metaphors abound.

Someone tried to convince me once that the candy cane that appears at Christmas time was developed with particular intentions in mind: the shape of the shepherd's crook, the red stripes reminding us of the Lord's scourging, the peppermint flavor reminiscent of the biblical plant hyssop, which Moses used to apply lamb's blood to the door lintels at the time of the Exodus, and so on. There does not seem to be any substantiation for these "investments of meaning." (The closest Christian connection I've been able to find for the candy cane is that a seventeenth-century music director at the Cologne Cathedral wanted to develop a treat that would keep the kids quiet while their parents rehearsed.) Yet the ideas work as a way to draw a connection between the Lord's birth and Passion.

Another example is the carol "The Twelve Days of Christmas." Perhaps you've heard the claim that it represents a clandestine catechism. Again, there is no substantiation for it being anything other than a whimsical song for the English celebration of "Twelfth Night." However, we can admire the sensitivity involved in drawing out new meanings for a Christian audience. For example, the "partridge in a pear tree" as a metaphor for the cross of Christ. The references include Jesus' self-identification with the image of the mother hen gathering her brood under her wings (Matthew 23:37); the apparent readiness of a mother partridge to sacrifice herself by feigning injury in order to draw predators away from her chicks; the wood of the cross becoming a tree of life, bearing fruit for all and so on. We human beings have quite a capacity to find and invest meaning wherever we look.

"Lift up your eyes on high and see...." The prophet Isaiah looked up into a starry night. The Babylonians, who had defeated and exiled the people of Israel, worshiped the stars. The stars were on their side. Isaiah looks up and sees something different. He sees God's army. He sees the God who transcends the stars. He knows that the God who called them and gave them a mission was their origin and destiny. To be in a covenant with the God of the stars would make a difference. They may be defeated, but

their hope will never run out. They may feel weary, but their strength will be renewed, and someday they'll soar like eagles.

The Babylonian Empire, like all empires, does fall. Isaiah's people remain strong in their identity and start to rebuild. The point of having contact with the transcendent God is not to wallow there beneath the stars. The point is to bring that "higher power" into our lives, into our problems, and to confront our obstacles.

> Come to me, all you that are weary and are carrying heavy burdens, and I will give you rest. Take my yoke upon you, and learn from me; for I am gentle and humble in heart, and you will find rest for your souls. For my yoke is easy, and my burden is light.
> (Matthew 11:28–30)

We see in Jesus' teaching that same, strong capacity to invest meaning and create metaphors. He looked everywhere and saw images of the kingdom of God breaking through to the world. He saw signs that would open people's hearts to that reality. Perhaps he saw two oxen yoked together, sharing their burden, creating a new and greater force, achieving something more than one alone could accomplish—a sign of the transcendent God coming to us, drawing close to us, calling us into a partnership that brings us into a new reality.

Maybe you can identify a time when you were away from the city lights and looked up into a clear night and were taken away by the awesomeness of the Milky Way. Think about that time. Maybe you feel a sense of perspective being there before the stars. You think about what it means to be on a very small planet amid that vastness and yet so preoccupied with your problems and selfishness. You question what meaning there could be in all this for you.

Maybe you also sense that the transcendent God is concerned for you, that the God of the universe knows you and cares about you. Through the revelation of Jesus, *"Come to me,"* you hear an invitation from God, who does not want to stay above you, but wants to be close to you. A God who wants to renew your strength—and see you soar.

First
Week

Advent Acting

Christ has no body but yours,
No hands, no feet on earth but yours,
Yours are the eyes with which he looks
compassion on this world,
Yours are the feet with which he walks to do good,
Yours are the hands with which he blesses all the world.
Yours are the hands, yours are the feet,
Yours are the eyes, you are his body.
Christ has no body now but yours.

—TERESA OF AVILA

One
Burn the Candle

· · · · · · ·

There was a time when, if I really liked a particular piece of clothing, say a shirt or sweater or tie, I would never wear it. I liked it so much I wouldn't wear it. Crazy, isn't it? It wasn't because there weren't appropriate occasions to wear these things. I guess it was because I didn't want them to get worn out. I wanted to preserve their specialness. But what happened instead is that they were so well preserved that they outlived their usefulness. At some point I'd go to find something I was saving and then it would be out of style. Or my tastes had changed, so that I didn't want to wear it anymore. Like I said, crazy.

Maybe this ran in my family. I remember a Christmas candle when I was young that never got lit. It was a very nice, pretty candle that would get packed away and would come back every year. One year, though, the candle came out and didn't seem very pretty anymore. There was a film of dust and dirt (I think the technical term is *crud*) all over it. So, eventually, it got pitched. It was thrown away without ever doing for us what it was supposed to do.

Now those are just clothes and candles. But are there other things in life, other places in life where that can happen? Are there things that are too precious to expose to real life? Things we're afraid might get soiled? Maybe the most beautiful parts of ourselves? Maybe our faith? Are the most truthful parts of us just like that beautiful family Bible that's stored on a shelf and never opened?

As God's chosen ones, holy and beloved, clothe
yourselves with compassion, kindness, humility,
meekness, and patience. Bear with one another and, if
anyone has a complaint against another, forgive each
other; just as the Lord has forgiven you, so you also
must forgive. Above all, clothe yourselves with love,
which binds everything together in perfect harmony.
(Colossians 3:12–14)

Second
Week

Faith has to get soiled. It has to get worn. The stories of our
faith are meant to be a living word. If the stories of faith get
filed away in the special drawer labeled "sacred," they become
distant. They become hard to relate to. They become removed
from the real world and lose their connection with real people
and situations. They become less real. Less stories of faith and
more like fairy tales. When they're out in the open, there's a
chance we'll see their significance and learn from them. When
they only come out on special occasions, they're less pressing,
less important, less relevant.

In the fifteenth year of the reign of Emperor Tiberius,
when Pontius Pilate was governor of Judea, and Herod
was ruler of Galilee, and his brother Philip ruler of
the region of Ituraea and Trachonitis, and Lysanias
ruler of Abilene, during the high priesthood of Annas
and Caiaphas, the word of God came to John son
of Zechariah in the wilderness. He went into all the
region around the Jordan, proclaiming a baptism of
repentance for the forgiveness of sins, as it is written in
the book of the words of the prophet Isaiah,
"The voice of one crying out in the wilderness:

'Prepare the way of the Lord,
make his paths straight.'" (Luke 3:1-4)

I wonder if things had already started to feel distant to Luke's community. He was writing toward the end of the first century, in the 80s (yes, just "80s"). People had heard the stories of Jesus for a while. Did they begin to feel more distant, less real, even then? Luke begins his Gospel making the point strongly that the events he's talking about are historical. He doesn't begin with the words "once upon a time." This is not a bedtime story to lull you to sleep. No, he begins setting the time and context of these events in the real world. This *happened* in human history. It wasn't that long ago. It happened when Tiberius was emperor, Pilate was governor, Herod was tetrarch, Caiaphas was high priest.

In the real world, God spoke. We heard his voice. And it wasn't in powerful political forces or influential religious leaders. It was in this wild man from the desert who said, *"Prepare the way of the Lord, make his paths straight."* Little did we know how urgent and real that message was—that it truly was our paths he was talking about, the paths we travel every day. It was in the messiness of our lives that the Lord would come.

The message for those who still hear these words is that God is still speaking. God's mysterious presence is at work in the real world. Our world. We can hear it and we can be part of that movement of the Spirit right where we are, right now. At this time in history, our time, God speaks: I am coming to you.

Two
Putting Things Off

A voice cries out:
"In the wilderness prepare the way of the LORD,
   make straight in the desert a highway for our God.
Every valley shall be lifted up,
   and every mountain and hill be made low;
the uneven ground shall become level,
   and the rough places a plain.
Then the glory of the LORD shall be revealed,
   and all people shall see it together,
      for the mouth of the LORD has spoken."
(Isaiah 40:3–5)

•   •   •   •   •   •   •

Is the purpose of a vision only to show us a possible future? Is it merely a glimpse of a reality that is always far off? Is its grandness only a source for stuttering contemplation? Or does it start as soon as we hear and see it?

Potential is a beautiful word. There is part of us that is not yet here; there is part of us that is in process. But when we speak only of our potential, do we give ourselves permission to continually put off our vision? Perhaps *capacity* is the better word to challenge ourselves. Potentials are for the future. Capacities are for now. We have the capacity to act now, to use our gifts now, to live now.

We don't have to put off living to some uncertain future. We don't have to wait till we graduate, or the mortgage is paid, or the kids are grown to find time for each other, to get straight with God, to do what's important.

What are we putting off? Service, celebration, love, prayer? We're all doing so much, many important things, but we're probably also doing many things that aren't important at all. We can do what we think we don't have time for. There's a way to make space for the things and the people who will make this Advent and Christmas what we hope they will be. We can make space for what is more important.

We can level the mountains now: the mountains of arrogance, selfishness, resentment, and judgment. We don't have to pull down others to feel good about ourselves. We don't have to inflate ourselves or pursue "things" to give us more value. We can contribute our gifts for the good of others. We can choose to care about those who suffer or those who go without the things we take for granted. We can choose to forgive, reconcile, serve, reach out. We can reach out to that person who is usually overlooked but who needs help. We can give our ear to the one who needs to be listened to.

We can also fill the valleys now: the valleys of self-doubt, fear, or anything that keeps us down or holds us back. We don't have to dwell in those valleys, feeling unimportant or powerless. We don't have to avoid confronting problems that seem beyond our control. We can fill those valleys. We're not in this alone. God is working with us. As Thomas Merton once said, "The smallest thing, touched by charity, is immediately transfigured and becomes sublime."[4] Certainly we have the capacity to do the smallest thing.

We can pray now. That doesn't mean changing our whole lifestyle. It means folding prayer into our regular activities. When driving or walking to your next appointment, instead of rushing, take it easy. Recognize God's gifts around you. When you're writing your Christmas cards, pray for your friends and relatives as you address the envelopes. When you're shopping for gifts for those you care about, pray for them. When you're wrapping their presents, give thanks for them. What a way to invest our chores with more meaning. What a way to show love to the people in our lives. Everything becomes an Advent activity during Advent.

> I thank my God every time I remember you, constantly praying with joy in every one of my prayers for all of you, because of your sharing in the gospel from the first day until now. I am confident of this, that the one who began a good work among you will bring it to completion by the day of Jesus Christ.
> (Philippians 1:3-6)

All this happens—mountains fall, valleys are raised, and the work begun in us is brought to completion—because God is acting, too. God spoke in our history, and God continues to speak to us in our real world. God inspires visions for us to embrace, sends invitations for us to accept. We can accept those invitations.

Three
Stand Up

It's that time of year when we'll be offered a dozen different versions of *A Christmas Carol*. The Dickens classic will be served up as a musical, a cartoon, a Bill Murray comedy. It's a story that makes us nostalgic and brings comfort. It also brings discomfort. Something in us knows we need to hear its message again and again.

Some things endure. Some stories don't get stale. Writing is a craft that occasionally rises to the level of art. It speaks beyond its own time and place—directly to the human heart.

There's another Dickens classic that isn't as familiar to us, but we'd recognize the first line: "It was the best of times. It was the worst of times." You know that from *A Tale of Two Cities*. The novel takes place during the French Revolution and exciting ideas are in the air: liberty, equality, fraternity. There's also a reign of terror going on: injustice is breeding injustice; oppression is breeding oppression. "It was the best of times. It was the worst of times." Those words sum up so much. We see the whole drama unfolding from there.

What about our own age? Are these the best of times or the worst of times? What do we see?

We might say that these are clearly the best of times. Look at what we can do. Look at advances in science and in health care. Life expectancies increase. Medical conditions that would have been death sentences in the past are now passages that can be negotiated. Regular folks today can live better than royalty or the super rich of past ages: lifestyle, conveniences, the goods we are able to buy and enjoy, the ease of travel, technologies that open up everything the world has to offer, information and entertainment at our finger tips. We can lead lives of discovery. We can know and enjoy more than any other generation in history. Our quality of life surely makes these the best of times.

But we could look at all those same areas and see something else. We hear other news, other stories: rising incidence of

degenerative disease, inaccessibility to good health care for
so many, ideological extremism, environmental degradation,
stress levels. The same power plants that bring us our energy
can leave hazardous waste. The same economic systems that
bring the goods of the world to us so inexpensively can prop
up oppression in other places. The same technologies that can
inform and entertain can harden and desensitize. The same
Internet that heals and brings the world together also harms and
tears the world apart. How easy it is now to foster evil intentions
and to export terror. Maybe these are the worst of times.

Every age could see itself that way. In every age people could
say they have the best and the worst to deal with right here.

> When you see Jerusalem surrounded by armies, then
> know that its desolation has come near. Then those in
> Judea must flee to the mountains, and those inside the
> city must leave it, and those out in the country must not
> enter it; for these are days of vengeance, as a fulfillment
> of all that is written. . . .
> "There will be signs in the sun, the moon, and the
> stars, and on the earth distress among nations confused
> by the roaring of the sea and the waves. People will
> faint from fear and foreboding of what is coming upon
> the world, for the powers of the heavens will be shaken.
> Then they will see the 'Son of Man coming in a cloud'
> with power and great glory. Now when these things
> begin to take place, stand up and raise your heads,
> because your redemption is drawing near.
> (Luke 21:20-22, 25-28)

Luke wrote to the early Christians, who knew what it was
like to be oppressed. Like their ancestors, they saw Jerusalem

*Second
Week*

destroyed again, this time by the Romans. They saw death, destruction, crises. They were scattered and uncertain of what was coming next. St. Luke gives them a context in which to see it all. He tells them to remember Jesus' prophetic words about the end times. He's telling them to apply those words to their crisis.

Those apocalyptic images speak to all our crises. The sun, the moon, the stars—the heavens are shaken. Have you ever felt like the world was crashing down around you? That your world was shaking? You didn't know what else you could do. You were caught in *"the roaring of the sea and the waves."*

If you haven't felt like that, you will someday. And the message we receive from Jesus is that when you have to go through these times, these crises, *"Stand up and raise your heads."*

Ultimately, what will make this the best or the worst of times for us is not how much we have, how many conveniences we enjoy, or even our geopolitical situation. What will determine our true quality of life will be how we respond, how we act in the midst of the crises, the problems, and the questions—how we respond to whatever life brings.

This is the season of Advent. We're reminded that our ransom is near. Our liberation is at hand. You can be full of hope, energy, and life. Because your hope is not based on what's around you. It's based in what the Lord has done for you and will do for you. You are not alone.

Four
Raise Your Heads

• • • • • • •

S tand up and raise your heads." (Luke 21:28). What a confident instruction from Jesus in Luke's Gospel. Others may cower and flee, but not you, he tells his disciples. But we know ourselves well enough to know that we are not always as confident and stalwart as that.

> And may the Lord make you increase and abound in love for one another and for all, just as we abound in love for you. And may he so strengthen your hearts in holiness that you may be blameless before our God and Father at the coming of our Lord Jesus with all his saints. (1 Thessalonians 3:12-13)

That's St. Paul's message to the Thessalonians. Many of them were frightened in the face of the challenges they faced. Some started to sit back and become complacent, as if they only needed to wait for Jesus to return. Paul points out how inappropriate that is for Christians. This is the time to go to work, he tells them. Look at the opportunities God is giving us to be true disciples here and now. He prays for them: *"May the Lord make you increase and abound in love for one another and for all."* That's our response. That's how we are to meet what life brings. By increasing and abounding in love.

Again, we are reminded of the Advent call to alert and active waiting. When we have to deal with our day-to-day problems, fears, deadlines, illnesses, the unknown, when we have to deal with big problems, with systems that exclude and abuse, with technologies that are misused, we do not become complacent or fearful. We do not cower. We need to ask: what is the loving thing to do? We need to stand up and raise our heads.

In a time when the world is confused about its values, we can stand up. We can build our lives on those values that last, that have withstood the test of time. We can witness to the values we receive from the gospel, values that embody wisdom, that are ever new and fresh and life giving. We don't have to be perfect, but we can keep finding our bearings in those values—and help others find the same.

When things are going well in our own lives, and we are tempted to become forgetful of others' needs, or we sit back and sedate ourselves and our hearts become complacent, we need to stand up and pray in gratitude. We need to be open to the opportunities God gives us in life, and seek ways to actively serve others with our strengths.

And yet even the most confident disciple knows the other side of the story. How much easier it is to disappear into the complacent crowd. How enticing not to stand out, or speak up, or be different. In our weariness, how tempting it is to sit on the sidelines while the fight for justice goes on, to waver in the battle against darkness.

> For a brief moment I abandoned you,
>   but with great compassion I will gather you.
> In overflowing wrath for a moment
>   I hid my face from you,
> but with everlasting love I will have compassion on you,
>   says the LORD, your Redeemer. . . .

For the mountains may depart
   and the hills be removed,
but my steadfast love shall not depart from you,
   and my covenant of peace shall not be removed,
   says the LORD, who has compassion on you.
(Isaiah 54:7–8, 10)

Some of Isaiah's prophecies came at a time when his people were thinking about their shortcomings and sins, their failures to keep their covenant with God. They confronted their mistaken policies and outright idolatries. They questioned how they could manage to be different in the future. Could they really change? Wouldn't their frailties keep getting in their way?

When we have to confront our own weakness and sin, when our personal problems seem insurmountable, when they are shaking our world, we stand up and remember that we can get through anything with God. We remember that God's unshakeable love always wants to give us the grace of a new start.

Advent is a time of expectation and preparation for the Lord's coming. It's a time of hope and trust in God's promises to us. New beginnings are possible. The best way for us to prepare, Jesus tells us, is to stand up, raise our heads, and be about the things he told us to be about. And when the Lord comes, we will recognize him and the liberation he brings.

Five
Jump

As Jesus went on from there, two blind men followed
him, crying loudly, "Have mercy on us, Son of David!"
When he entered the house, the blind men came to
him; and Jesus said to them, "Do you believe that I am
able to do this?" They said to him, "Yes, Lord." Then he
touched their eyes and said, "According to your faith let
it be done to you." And their eyes were opened. Then
Jesus sternly ordered them, "See that no one knows of
this." But they went away and spread the news about
him throughout that district.
(Matthew 9:27–31)

• • • • • • •

In this small episode from Matthew's Gospel, two men follow
Jesus asking for a healing. We're told they are crying out to
him. He must have heard, but we get the impression that he
keeps on walking. And they keep on following. That could not
have been easy for them if they were blind. Were they listening
for his voice, his steps, for some indication of the direction he
was going? Why would Jesus act this way toward the men?

This story is as much about discipleship as it is about healing.
When Jesus gets to his destination, he finally acknowledges
them and says, *"Do you believe that I am able to do this?"* He has seen
their desire, their persistence, their confidence. He has, in a
way, forced them to show it. You can't be a disciple without
that belief, that confidence in him. You won't be able to follow
him for the rest of journey down that road without having your
belief tested, challenged, refined.

"Do you believe that I am able to do this?" He gives them another chance to show him that confidence, to say again what is in their hearts. And he gives them a chance to reconsider. As if to say: Do you really want this? Are you sure you're ready for the responsibility that this gift will bring? Because with every gift comes responsibility. We are given the charge to use every gift for the good of ourselves and others for God's glory.

A friend of mine once told me about his desire to go back to school to finish a degree. If he didn't, he said, there was very little chance that he could keep progressing in his field. He wouldn't get any promotions and would languish where he was. He really wanted to have that degree and all it would offer him. His current company was even going to help him get it. But he lacked confidence. He was afraid to do it. He rehearsed with me all the reasons the effort wasn't worth it: the money it would cost, the time it would take. He thought it would take five years for him to get the degree while working full time. He said, "Do you know how old I'll be in five years?" You can guess my response: "Same age you'll be if you don't get the degree?"

For someone else in other circumstances, going back to school may have been the wrong decision. For him, it turned out to be the right one. He came to know that because of his willingness to stay on the road and keep listening to that deep desire within. At some point we may come to that conclusion: "I see what I have to do. It's not going to be easy. Part of me is scared. But I'm going to do it. Here I go!"

Can you think of times in your life when you were at such a point? Perhaps you didn't act and you regret it. Perhaps you jumped and you are grateful for all it has meant to your life. Perhaps you jumped and things didn't turn out as you expected,

but maybe you learned things you wouldn't have otherwise. You
saw the path before you in a new way.

> Shall not Lebanon in a very little while
>   become a fruitful field,
>   and the fruitful field be regarded as a forest?
> On that day the deaf shall hear
>   the words of a scroll,
> and out of their gloom and darkness
>   the eyes of the blind shall see.
> The meek shall obtain fresh joy in the LORD,
>   and the neediest people shall exult in the Holy One
>   of Israel. (Isaiah 29:17–19)

Faith is a gift we are invited to receive. The Scriptures invite
us to have confidence in God. The prophets promise a new kind
of hearing and a new kind of sight that will allow us to perceive
the bounty around us and rejoice in it. It is a gift that is worth
crying out for when the one who offers it is passing by.

Faith is a gift, but it is one we have to apply. When we've
got it, it's like a muscle that needs to be used. It needs to be
nourished with prayer and exercised in action and risk. A good
Advent exercise might be to actually think about the gifts you've
been given. Write them down. Are you using them for God?

We are good at asking for gifts from God. Do we also thank
God for all that has already been given? For the health we have
and the healing that has been worked in us? For the jumps we
were able to take and the confidence to jump again?

Six
On the Prowl

An account of the genealogy of Jesus the Messiah, the
son of David, the son of Abraham.

   Abraham was the father of Isaac, and Isaac the
father of Jacob, and Jacob the father of Judah and his
brothers. . . . (Matthew 1:1-2)

* * * * * * *

Have you had this experience before? You're going through
a really tough time. You feel abandoned and alone. And
you feel that not even God is paying attention. You ask, "Where
are you God? Don't you care that I'm going through all this?"

Then, later—it could be weeks, months, years—you look
back over that time and begin to see how God was there. The
Lord's hand was at work. The Lord was putting the right people
on your path, bringing about your good. You couldn't see it back
then, when you were in the middle of it. But when you look back,
you have a new perspective. You see the bigger picture.

Theology has a name for that kind of experience. It's *prevenient
grace*, the grace that is always, already there. It's the name for
how God prepares us for grace, how God's action enlightens
and readies us to receive his gift. God graces us to say yes to
grace. And when we say yes, it's because God has given us the
wisdom and strength to do it.

St. Matthew includes a genealogy of Jesus in the first chapter
of his Gospel. It is a long list of Jesus' ancestors; yet it's more
of a theological statement than a literal one. We can see this,
since St. Luke also includes a genealogy of Jesus that differs in
some ways. Luke has a different theological point to make. Both

of them are concerned with showing the workings of God's grace throughout the history of the chosen people, preparing humanity to receive the Messiah. It's by looking back on that history, in light of the experience of Jesus, that we see how God was working.

> Then Jacob called his sons, and said: "Gather around, that I may tell you what will happen to you in days to come.
> Assemble and hear, O sons of Jacob;
>> listen to Israel your father. . . .
> Judah, your brothers shall praise you;
>> your hand shall be on the neck of your enemies;
>> your father's sons shall bow down before you.
> Judah is a lion's whelp;
>> from the prey, my son, you have gone up.
> He crouches down, he stretches out like a lion,
>> like a lioness—who dares rouse him up?
> The scepter shall not depart from Judah,
>> nor the ruler's staff from between his feet,
> until tribute comes to him;
>> and the obedience of the peoples is his."
> (Genesis 49:1-2, 8-10)

Jesus traces his lineage to Judah, to the royal house of Israel. Jacob used the image of a lion for his son Judah, the image of strength, power, and beauty in nature. The Messiah is known as the "lion of Judah." He is on the prowl, working in the silence of human history, working on our behalf, to prepare us for himself, for a new life.

What about our personal histories? What in our own history, stories, or families has been preparing us for the coming of the

Messiah? In what ways has he been on the prowl, ready to answer our cries, our hope? Even in the darkest times, when we thought God was far from us, how has the Lord been there, preparing? Inviting us to another place, showing us another path?

Coming to see how the Lord has worked in our history prepares us for meeting him in our future as well. Silent, powerful. Ready to care for us in our need. We come to know that, even in the tough times, we can have hope. The Lord will not abandon us. That's part of the message of Advent: grace is among us, always there, preparing the way.

Seven
An Everlasting Rock

"Everyone then who hears these words of mine and acts on them will be like a wise man who built his house on rock. The rain fell, the floods came, and the winds blew and beat on that house, but it did not fall, because it had been founded on rock. And everyone who hears these words of mine and does not act on them will be like a foolish man who built his house on sand. The rain fell, and the floods came, and the winds blew and beat against that house, and it fell—and great was its fall!"

Now when Jesus had finished saying these things, the crowds were astounded at his teaching, for he taught them as one having authority, and not as their scribes. (Matthew 7:24–29)

I magine someone whose house is falling apart. The plumbing is springing leaks. Doors and windows are coming out of alignment. Cracks are developing in concrete slabs. At first, the owner sets out to hire a plumber and handyman to fix the leaks and adjust the windows and patch the cracks. But the problems persist and multiply. Patching is not enough. Finally, an engineer is called in and determines there is a foundational problem. People will have to move out so that more extensive work can be done, work on a new foundation. It's going to take time and expense, but there's no other way to save the structure.

Is your house falling apart? After dealing again and again with the same personal problems, relationship problems, bad decisions, financial troubles, ruts, addictions—some people begin to realize that patching won't work anymore. They begin to see that somewhere along the way they established a bad foundation. They didn't take the time to build well. Their house is unsafe. They need to commit to building something new, piece by piece. They need a new beginning. It will take time, but it will be worth it.

All our lives, we are building. What is it like to build on rock? What is some of the work that needs to happen?

First of all, there is inner work. We need to know ourselves deeply. This is also the beginning of prayer. It requires going within, searching within, being honest with ourselves. In time, with a listening ear to God's voice within, understanding comes. Self-awareness and acceptance come.

There is also the work of seeking community. We are called to share the journey we are on. Think of all those who are lighting Advent candles with us this season: those who are close to us and those who are far off. We are on the same path. As we share ourselves with others we are able both to give help to them and to receive support from them. So often it is in community that we learn about the values that last. Not the most convenient values, but the values that last, because they tell us the truth about ourselves and about life.

And there is the work of applying what we learn. St. Paul, in his letter to the Philippians, instructs the members of his church: *"Keep on doing the things that you have learned and received and heard and seen in me"* (4:9). Heard and seen. His words are not enough. They need his example.

That is what is meant by the "living tradition" of Christianity. It is how the gospel is passed on and deepened in the community. We don't express our faith just in words, but in the example of our lives. We don't merely or blindly accept teachings; we open our minds to understand the values behind those teachings, which we can then express in our own circumstances.

One who hears the Word must put it into practice. In that way we are applying what we learn. We are building on rock.

> On that day this song will be sung in the land of Judah:
> We have a strong city;
> > he sets up victory
> > like walls and bulwarks.
> Open the gates,
> > so that the righteous nation that keeps faith
> > may enter in.
> Those of steadfast mind you keep in peace—
> > in peace because they trust in you.
> Trust in the LORD forever,
> > for in the LORD GOD
> > you have an everlasting rock. (Isaiah 26:1–4)

As we apply our faith in practical ways, we are becoming more like that city that Isaiah describes to his people: powerful, but not a closed fortress. Its gates are open to receive what is good all around us. We are willing to learn more about what really works in life, what is righteous.

Storms will come—the tempests of human failure and disappointment, those problems and disasters that make us feel like our house is falling apart. But with this foundation, not only will we pass through those times and survive, but we will also become stronger because of them. We do not depend just on ourselves and what is passing. We have a foundation of trust in the Lord, the everlasting rock.

John's Call

[It may] reasonably be maintained that the true object
of all human life is play. Earth is a task garden; heaven
is a playground. To be at last in such secure innocence
that one can juggle the universe and the stars, to be
so good that one can treat everything as a joke—that
may be the real end and final holiday of human souls.
When we are really holy we may regard the Universe
as a lark.

—G. K. CHESTERTON

One
Roots

The days are surely coming, says the LORD, when I will fulfill the promise I made to the house of Israel and the house of Judah. In those days and at that time I will cause a righteous Branch to spring up for David; and he shall execute justice and righteousness in the land. In those days Judah will be saved and Jerusalem will live in safety. And this is the name by which it will be called: "The LORD is our righteousness." (Jeremiah 33:14–16)

• • • • • • •

Someone told me a story about an Italian-American man who was on a trip to Italy. While he was there, he made a side trip to the old village of his ancestors. He wanted to get in touch with his roots. And he loved it, because it was everything he had imagined it would be. It was a bustling little place, but everyone seemed to know each other.

While in this village, he visited the church in the center of town. Even though it was a small village, in the piazza there was a huge church, a basilica. He walked around inside the empty church, admiring all the art. But then he was distracted by a noise coming from the back. He looked and saw a little boy playing. Now, this boy wasn't playing in the way you'd usually see a kid carrying on in church. This boy was actually playing ball. He was bouncing a ball off a wall and the sound was echoing loudly throughout the church.

At first the man tried to ignore it, but then he got more and more annoyed. He looked around, but didn't see any parents. He began to wonder, what kind of parents let their kid go wild

in a sacred place like this? So, he went to the back of the church
and walked up to the boy. In his broken Italian he said: "Hey,
what do you think you're doing? This is a church! What's wrong
with you? Don't you know how to act in here?"

The boy just looked at him, puzzled. Finally, he replied, "This
is my father's house."

The man was stopped in his tracks. He didn't know if this kid
was just a study in cultural differences, or if he meant his father
was the sacristan, or if he was spouting profound theology. But
right then his whole idea about being there changed. He had
been approaching the place as he would a museum. Then he
remembered that he was in his Father's house.

All the art and beauty we invest in a church building, all the
reverence we have for it, the approach we have to liturgy, the
careful attention we give to sacred rites—all of those things
—are not ends in themselves. And they are not meant to be
idolized. They point to something. They point to the relationships, the meaning, the love we bring there as people of faith.
Think of the beautiful lights, music, and décor churches invest
in during the Advent and Christmas seasons. It all points to the
experience of Christ we can have there.

A shoot shall come out from the stump of Jesse,
    and a branch shall grow out of his roots.
The spirit of the LORD shall rest on him,
    the spirit of wisdom and understanding,
    the spirit of counsel and might,
    the spirit of knowledge and the fear of the LORD.
His delight shall be in the fear of the LORD.
(Isaiah 11:1–3)

You've probably heard the expression about finding one's "roots and wings." Roots give us grounding, identity, security. That's so we can use our wings, so we can go out and live full lives, tackling obstacles, meeting challenges. Without roots, we're scattered, directionless.

The prophets Isaiah and Jeremiah both talk about roots. They write at a time of uncertainty and flux, a time of defeat for their people. A foreign nation has taken away their home, destroyed their temple. They've been reduced to nothing. They were once a great tree, but someone came and took an ax to it and chopped it down.

When you think life is over, there's hope in the roots. The roots remind us of who we are. Remember the Spirit that makes us a people, Isaiah says. It's because of that Spirit that a shoot shall sprout from that stump. Something new will come of this. A surge of new life will fill you and you will be a new people. You will be great again, but not as in the past. It will be different. It will be better because of what you've been through. You will know spiritual greatness.

Where do we remember our roots: who we are, where we've come from, and the power of life within us? Where's our home base? Are we "at home" in our Father's house?

Home is a place where people reach out to one another. If we don't want to really know one another at church, how could it be a home? We're not called to be a community of strangers. We're called to share the journey together. That means sharing ourselves. Home is a place where we can play together. It's a place where you hate to miss a party. We look for excuses to get together.

Home is a place where we are nourished, in body and soul. We eat together. We learn to pray together. We learn from the

Scriptures and the spiritual traditions of our church that have
been handed down to us. We search through our questions
together. The journey of faith sometimes requires searching,
and learning from each other's experiences.

Home is a place of mercy. It's a place where we are ready to
share each other's burdens and to give and receive support. I
remember hearing an interview with Rachel Naomi Remen,
the founder of an organization called Commonweal, which
gives retreats for terminally ill people. I remember one line
especially: "We all have pain," she said, "but here we don't hide
it…and so we learn to trust." There's no home without trust,
through good times and bad.

There is a quote from another Italian boy, Angelo Roncalli,
who became Pope John XXIII: "We are not here on earth to
guard a museum. We are here to cultivate a flourishing garden
of life." Cultivating a garden means getting our hands dirty.
We may have to get into the dirt and manure to learn to love,
understand, and forgive each other. It's within our messiness
that we allow ourselves to share our burdens and grow from
our mistakes.

It would not be appropriate to have a softball game in the
sanctuary of your church. But it would be an even greater
scandal if your church became a museum: nice and clean, and
barren and lifeless, no one learning from their mistakes, no
one learning how to love.

We are getting ready to celebrate the Feast of the Incarnation.
The Lord made a home with us. What better time is there to
embrace our home? Now is the time to commit to the vision of
our church as a garden where trees bear fruit. It's a place where
we find roots and wings, where we challenge one another to
live Jesus' vision in all areas of life, and take him to the world.

Then every pew, every window, every work of art in that church will be shouting that we're in our Father's house, that we're home.

Two
Wings

· · · · · · ·

Home is a place where we are planted, rooted. The more rooted we are, though, the more free we become. We're rooted in acceptance. We're rooted in a freedom that calls us to be ourselves. We're free to explore who we are, to be honest with ourselves and each other. When we accept each other as we are, we prepare ourselves for surprises, for change, for newness of life. Our roots become wings.

In the days of King Herod of Judea, there was a priest named Zechariah, who belonged to the priestly order of Abijah. His wife was a descendant of Aaron, and her name was Elizabeth. Both of them were righteous before God, living blamelessly according to all the commandments and regulations of the Lord. But they had no children, because Elizabeth was barren, and both were getting on in years.

Once when he was serving as priest before God and his section was on duty, he was chosen by lot, according to the custom of the priesthood, to enter the sanctuary of the Lord and offer incense. Now at the

time of the incense offering, the whole assembly of the
people was praying outside. Then there appeared to
him an angel of the Lord, standing at the right side of
the altar of incense. When Zechariah saw him, he was
terrified; and fear overwhelmed him. But the angel said
to him, "Do not be afraid, Zechariah, for your prayer
has been heard. Your wife Elizabeth will bear you a
son, and you will name him John. You will have joy
and gladness, and many will rejoice at his birth, for
he will be great in the sight of the Lord. He must never
drink wine or strong drink; even before his birth he will
be filled with the Holy Spirit. He will turn many of the
people of Israel to the Lord their God. With the spirit
and power of Elijah he will go before him, to turn the
hearts of parents to their children, and the disobedient
to the wisdom of the righteous, to make ready a people
prepared for the Lord." (Luke 1:5–17)

Zechariah, the priest, enters the sanctuary, the symbol of the
people's "home" with God, the center of their faith and way
of life, of everything that holds them together as a people. It's
there that he's asked to sprout wings. Like Abraham and Sarah
before them, Zechariah and Elizabeth are being called to something
new. It's never too late to answer that call, to respond to
the subtle and deep invitations that life brings. God is inviting
us to fly, to serve in a new way.

Elizabeth and Zechariah, as elders, discover their unique role.
They must provide a home for a prophet, the forerunner to the
Messiah. Surely this is too much at this time of their lives. How
can they answer such a call? How can they manage moving their
lives in such a new direction? Whatever God calls us to do, we

will find those wings. Whenever the divine invitation comes, it will be the right time.

A friend of mine began writing seriously after his seventieth birthday. Now he's invited to speak to groups about his experiences. God is using the richness of his spirituality to inspire and teach others. Another friend decided to answer a call at her church to volunteer at a juvenile detention center. She never thought of herself doing this before. Now she has become the coordinator of the ministry. She says she receives so much more from her outreach than she gives. A whole new life has opened up for her.

> Welcome one another, therefore, just as Christ has welcomed you, for the glory of God. For I tell you that Christ has become a servant of the circumcised on behalf of the truth of God in order that he might confirm the promises given to the patriarchs, and in order that the Gentiles might glorify God for his mercy. As it is written, "Therefore I will confess you among the Gentiles, and sing praises to your name." (Romans 15:7-9)

In his letter to the Romans, St. Paul is writing to two groups. One is more powerful, one is weaker. One is of Gentile origin, the other has a Jewish background. They are trying to build a new "home" together, but there is dissention. There is tension and disagreement about customs and interpretations. Paul says to them: "*Welcome one another . . . as Christ has welcomed you*" (another translation: "*Accept one another . . . as Christ accepted you*" NIV).

He's telling them: We're building something new here. We're building it on the kind of acceptance Christ shows us. It goes deeper than any differences we have. Christ came to us where we are, and so we have the power to move, to change. Even when we need to work through our differences, there is a source of unity and harmony in what we share. We may not agree on everything, but we can still accept each other.

Home is not always going to be a nice, sweet, comfy experience. When all the other pieces are in place, and when acceptance is present, we can often finally hear the real challenge that others bring to our lives.

In those days John the Baptist appeared in the wilderness of Judea, proclaiming, "Repent, for the kingdom of heaven has come near." . . . Then the people of Jerusalem and all Judea were going out to him, and all the region along the Jordan, and they were baptized by him in the river Jordan, confessing their sins.

But when he saw many Pharisees and Sadducees coming for baptism, he said to them, "You brood of vipers! Who warned you to flee from the wrath to come? Bear fruit worthy of repentance. Do not presume to say to yourselves, 'We have Abraham as our ancestor'; for I tell you, God is able from these stones to raise up children to Abraham. Even now the ax is lying at the root of the trees; every tree therefore that does not bear good fruit is cut down and thrown into the fire.

"I baptize you with water for repentance, but one who is more powerful than I is coming after me; I am not worthy to carry his sandals. He will baptize you with the Holy Spirit and fire. His winnowing fork is in his hand, and he will clear his threshing floor and will

gather his wheat into the granary; but the chaff he will
burn with unquenchable fire." (Matthew 3:1-2, 5-12)

John the Baptist is not very "nice" in this passage. He calls
people snakes, useless branches to be burned. It's not enough to
say Abraham is our father. It's not enough to go to the church
office and produce a baptism certificate. An ax is coming. It is
ready to strike at the roots, to cut away anything that is lifeless
in us. God does not want to fit comfortably into our schedule.
God wants to be a living presence in our lives, fire in our hearts.

When we're really "at home" with one another we can go
beyond "niceness" to a challenge we can really hear. We can
say: "Because I know you and care about you, I can see you're
getting into trouble." Or we can say: "I see more in you. I see
the gifts and talents you aren't using. What's keeping you from
using them? You can do better. You can be more." We're able
to offer those words, or listen to others who bring difficult and
challenging words to us, when we sense where those words are
coming from. They must be grounded in our love and care for
each other.

Love makes a deeper openness and a deeper harmony possible.
It's that love that allows us to draw strength from one another.
Then "home" lights a fire in us, and gives us wings.

Three
Point the Way

Get you up to a high mountain,
O Zion, herald of good tidings;
lift up your voice with strength,
O Jerusalem, herald of good tidings,
lift it up, do not fear;
say to the cities of Judah,
"Here is your God!" (Isaiah 40:9)

* * * * * * *

There is a saying attributed to Confucius: "The wise one points to the moon; the foolish one stares at the finger." That raises an Advent question for me. Where are our lives pointing? To ourselves? Beyond ourselves?

Each of the Gospel authors begins the presentation of Jesus' ministry with the preaching of John the Baptist—it's that important to them. They want to remember the one whom God chose to prepare the way, the one who emphatically pointed to Jesus. That may be because that's our role, too. It's the role of every Christian. God chooses us to prepare the Lord's way in our time and place, in our lives, words, actions. That's where we do our "pointing."

The beginning of the good news of Jesus Christ, the Son of God.
As it is written in the prophet Isaiah,
"See, I am sending my messenger ahead of you,
who will prepare your way;
the voice of one crying out in the wilderness:

'Prepare the way of the Lord,
make his paths straight.'" (Mark 1:1-3)

Mark's Gospel begins with the words: *"The beginning of the good news of Jesus Christ, the Son of God."* In Greek the word for *gospel* is *evangelion*. Mark is the only one of the four Evangelists to use that word in the title of his book. He's saying: "This is the *evangelion!*" which means "this is the Good News that I'm proclaiming to you!" In the midst of our experience, in the midst of human struggles, doubts, and fears, in the midst of our hopes, dreams, aspirations, we've got this Good News. God has sent us Good News.

Is that what we proclaim in our lives? Are we telling others that we've got Good News? How many Christians, instead of *preparing* the Lord's way, *get in* the Lord's way? We make it harder for others to find the Lord. We proclaim bad news.

What idea of our faith do people get when they look at us? Are we about mere obligation? Debilitating fear? False guilt? Or do they see the faith that casts out fear with love and openness, the faith that transforms duty into delight and obligation into freedom, the faith that feeds our desire to do good and to fulfill our purpose? Do they see the faith that obliterates false guilt, the guilt people use to beat themselves, and allows a healthy sense of guilt to do its proper job at the proper time, getting us back on track to being our best selves? Do they see the faith that brings true awareness and humility into our lives, and widens our perspective to see more than we can without it?

Do they see the faith that is most of all about joy? This is a joy that stays with us and accompanies us even through the toughest times of our lives, because it is rooted in the Resurrection. The only way we can proclaim the Good News to others is to experience it ourselves. It is only when we know how good that Good News is that we will share it. We need to keep evangelizing ourselves. We need to keep going to that Good News so we experience it and live from it.

Christians don't have to be perfect, but they need to know what it is like to be forgiven, redeemed, loved. We need to know what it's like to be graced and embraced by God. That's what changes us and makes a difference in the way we act in the world. When others see that, their interest is piqued, their questions and hopes are awakened, and they say: "What is this *evangelion*, this message, this faith they have?" And we are preparing the way.

> John the baptizer appeared in the wilderness,
> proclaiming a baptism of repentance for the
> forgiveness of sins. And people from the whole
> Judean countryside and all the people of Jerusalem
> were going out to him, and were baptized by him
> in the river Jordan, confessing their sins. Now
> John was clothed with camel's hair, with a leather
> belt around his waist, and he ate locusts and wild
> honey. (Mark 1:4-6)

John wore "camel's hair" and fed on "locusts and wild honey." I don't think the honey helps that image much. And this wasn't a nice camel hair jacket, either. It probably smelled bad and had gnats running around in it. This is not someone you'd want to invite to your next dinner party. But this tells us John knew how to strip away the nonessentials, those same nonessentials that cloud our vision. He was close to the earth, down to earth. He didn't care what Herod or the Pharisees or the high priest thought of him. He saw through all that. He didn't need to be like them or liked by them. He knew who he was.

People left Jerusalem and flocked to the desert to hear him because they recognized that he was real thing. Here the message and the living matched. The more we let go of the masks, the lies, the game playing, the need for others' approval, the false pride—the more real we are. That's what Spirit does for us: the Spirit makes us more real.

And that's what God uses. We bring the Lord our authentic selves, who we really are, and the Lord will use that authenticity for others. The more we are our true selves, the more we can point beyond ourselves to the truth beyond us. The more we prepare the Lord's way.

> He proclaimed, "The one who is more powerful than I is coming after me; I am not worthy to stoop down and untie the thong of his sandals. I have baptized you with water; but he will baptize you with the Holy Spirit." (Mark 1:7-8)

John keeps pointing to Jesus. He proclaims that Jesus is the one who will *"baptize you with the Holy Spirit."* The word *baptism* literally means to "immerse." He will immerse you in the Holy Spirit. Do you want Good News? Christ will immerse you in Good News. It's going to be coming out of your ears when you get to know him, his love, his Spirit. That's what fills us and changes us.

What do we do to prepare the way? We allow ourselves to be who we truly are. We allow ourselves to be forgiven and loved. We point to that Spirit, that love that makes a difference in our lives and empowers us to make a difference in the world.

Four
Knowing Who You Aren't

• • • • • • •

The movie *Rudy* is a fun sports tale. And there is a great line in it. Rudy, this Notre Dame student and football player, is going through a hard time. He's confused, carrying the weight of the world on himself. He talks to a professor of his, a priest named Fr. Cavanaugh. As part of his advice, Fr. Cavanaugh says: "Son, in thirty five years of religious study, I have only come up with two hard, incontrovertible facts: there is a God, and I'm not him."

That reminds me of John the Baptist. He knew who he wasn't.

> There was a man sent from God, whose name was John. He came as a witness to testify to the light, so that all might believe through him. He himself was not the light, but he came to testify to the light . . . This is the testimony given by John when the Jews sent priests and Levites from Jerusalem to ask him, "Who are you?" He confessed and did not deny it, but confessed, "I am not the Messiah." And they asked him, "What then? Are you Elijah?" He said, "I am not." "Are you the prophet?" He answered, "No." Then they said to him, "Who are you? Let us have an answer for those who sent us. What do you say about yourself?" He said,
>
> "I am the voice of one crying out in the wilderness,
> 'Make straight the way of the Lord,'"
>
> as the prophet Isaiah said.
>
> Now they had been sent from the Pharisees. They asked him, "Why then are you baptizing if you are

neither the Messiah, nor Elijah, nor the prophet?" John answered them, "I baptize with water. Among you stands one whom you do not know, the one who is coming after me; I am not worthy to untie the thong of his sandal." This took place in Bethany across the Jordan where John was baptizing.
(John 1:6–8, 19–28)

When they ask him, *"Who are you?"* the first thing John says is: *"I am not the Messiah."* (Maybe today we would say he didn't have a "messiah complex.")

He knew who he wasn't: not Elijah, not Moses. And, he knew who he was: *"I am the voice of one crying out in the wilderness, 'Make straight the way of the Lord.'"*

He's saying: I'm here to prepare the way and to make it a highway. I want to make it easier for people to go on that journey to meet the Lord. I want to make it easier for that encounter to happen. I want to pave the way for the Lord who is coming into the world and into our lives.

John the Baptist accepted himself. He was true to himself. He understood his role. He wasn't trying to be something he was not. And it was that self-knowledge that opened up a profound sense of mission, an awareness of God's personal call.

We need to know who we are and who we aren't (or else we might fall into our own messiah complexes). We aren't God, although sometimes we like to play God. We do that by passing judgment on one another, thinking we're all-important, thinking we have all the answers. We take more credit than we deserve. We amass our own kingdoms.

Or, we feel the weight of the whole world on ourselves. We think we have to fix everything, solve all the problems, make everybody happy. It's all up to us, our willpower, our intellect, our time. And it all results in a false perfectionism, arrogance, or anxiety. We end up doing violence to ourselves and others. We end up making a bigger mess of things.

Third
Week

It comes down to knowing who we are and who we aren't. One of the roles of the Messiah is just that: to show us the way to our true identity, to show us the way to ourselves. To show us what it means to be fully human.

Come to know yourself better and you will be able to know others better as well. Be happy with who you are and who you aren't. You will see more clearly the One who gave you your true self.

> As they went away, Jesus began to speak to the crowds about John: "What did you go out into the wilderness to look at? A reed shaken by the wind? What then did you go out to see? Someone dressed in soft robes? Look, those who wear soft robes are in royal palaces. What then did you go out to see? A prophet? Yes, I tell you, and more than a prophet. This is the one about whom it is written,
>
>   'See, I am sending my messenger ahead of you,
>   who will prepare your way before you.'
>
> Truly I tell you, among those born of women no one has arisen greater than John the Baptist; yet the least in the kingdom of heaven is greater than he. From the days of John the Baptist until now the kingdom of heaven has suffered violence, and the violent take it by force. For all the prophets and the law prophesied until John came; and if you are willing to accept it, he is Elijah who is to come. Let anyone with ears listen! (Matthew 11:7-15)

What great esteem Jesus held for his cousin John. He sees more in him than John himself does.

John refused to identify himself with Elijah in a literal way. Yet Jesus is free to identify John with Elijah metaphorically. He echoes what the angel said of John before he was born: that he would move in the *"spirit and power of Elijah"* (Luke 1:17). John points the way to the salvation that will be found only in Christ. What a glorious mission, for him and for us. It is in that role that our true selves shine. When we know who we are, we can point beyond ourselves to the source of our life, the source of our true identity. Those who have the ears to hear will begin to understand.

We are not the messiah. We can't save anybody. But we can be human. We can point to the source of salvation. We can strip away the illusions (and the little messiah complexes) that get in our way. We can bring our struggles and pain to the Lord, and we can send others to him. We can pave the way. We can make it easier for others to walk that road. We may feel like a voice in the wilderness at times. We may get dry in the desert, tired on the road. But the message of Advent tells us the Lord will be coming down that highway to meet us.

Five
Already and Not Yet

Say to those who are of a fearful heart,
  "Be strong, do not fear!
Here is your God.
  He will come with vengeance,
with terrible recompense.
  He will come and save you."

Then the eyes of the blind shall be opened,
  and the ears of the deaf unstopped;
then the lame shall leap like a deer,
  and the tongue of the speechless sing for joy.
(Isaiah 35:4-6)

• • • • • • •

We've already spoken about the spiritual value of patience, and the difference in Advent waiting. It calls forth from us endurance and attunes us to God's timetable. It fosters our growth and deepens our readiness to receive. But there's another message in the Scriptures:

When John heard in prison what the Messiah was
doing, he sent word by his disciples and said to him,
"Are you the one who is to come, or are we to wait for
another?" Jesus answered them, "Go and tell John what
you hear and see: the blind receive their sight, the lame
walk, the lepers are cleansed, the deaf hear, the dead
are raised, and the poor have good news brought to
them." (Matthew 11:2-5)

A strong message in the Gospels seems to be that your waiting is over. The kingdom is here. What do you see? The blind recover their sight. The lame walk. The deaf hear. The dead are raised. The poor have the Good News preached to them. These are signs that the kingdom has come. The new age, the messianic age has dawned. You can see it! It's happening! Now! At one place Jesus says the kingdom is *"at hand."* You can reach out and grab it any time you want.

Well, which is it? Do we have to wait, or is the waiting over?

Some theologians have an expression when they talk about Jesus' teaching on the kingdom of God. They call it "the already and the not yet." The kingdom is already here. But the kingdom is not yet here. Both are true. It's not a mixed message. It's a both/and. There's a certain kind of tension in this, and we live in that tension.

What does that tension look like for us—to live in the "already," but "not yet"? We wait for many things in life, some small (a vacation, a raise) and some big. What are the big things we wait for? The ability to love in a deeper way? The time when we won't fall into the same old traps we always do? A new vision for our lives? A change of heart? Is there a way we have these even as we await them?

John the Baptist is experiencing some of this tension when he sends his disciples to question Jesus. He's in prison and he sends a message asking, *"Are you the one who is to come, or are we to wait for another?"*

John had already said before being arrested, "Here is the Lamb of God—this is the one!" But now he's wondering again. He doesn't fully understand. That sounds very human. Can we relate to that? We know, we believe, yet... we wonder.

Some suggest that John is confused by the difference, the uniqueness of Jesus' teaching. It's not what he expected. John was a prophet of doom who was focused on repentance. Jesus is a prophet of salvation. Jesus doesn't live in the desert, he lives with people. He goes to feasts. He talks about God's kingdom as a wedding banquet! It's a message about God's favor, God's healing. It's Good News to the poor, to those who need it.

So Jesus says: Go to John and tell him what you see. The blind see, the lame walk, the dead are raised. The signs of the kingdom are here, all around me. The kingdom is breaking through *now* through *me*. There's no more waiting.

In biblical times, there were those who saw the blind, the poor, the lame not merely as unfortunate, but as cursed because of their sin. You wanted to stay away from them, remove them. Jesus comes and says that in the kingdom, the blind, the lame, the poor are loved, included, freed. God's love changes everything. It's happening right here and now.

We live in a certain tension. Where do we see it? What parts of ourselves do we wish weren't there? In what failures, weaknesses, or wrongdoing do we feel cursed? These are the places where new insights can break through. We come to see that our vulnerability is a gift, or that a weakness can be a strength. We come to know that the only love that is meaningful is the love that sees us as we are and loves us as we are.

Be patient, therefore, beloved, until the coming of the Lord. The farmer waits for the precious crop from the earth, being patient with it until it receives the early and the late rains. You also must be patient. Strengthen your hearts, for the coming of the Lord is near.
(James 5:7–8)

We live in tension. We live in the "both/and." The fullness of the kingdom is not here. It is coming. We need patience with ourselves and others. And yet...the kingdom is here. It is within us and all around us:

We're blinded by prejudice, narrowness, or self-doubt—but then a new experience opens our minds and lets in some light. We carry heavy burdens in life that keep us stuck, immobilized, lame—but then something or someone helps us to find the strength to move forward. We feel emotionally or spiritually poor—and the Good News of acceptance and love breaks through to us. We feel like we've come to a dead end, done in by destructive patterns in our lives—and then grace opens a door, showing us a new path.

And so the kingdom of God is here and now. The messianic age has dawned. We don't have to wait for a better time, or to find the perfect relationship, or to overcome all our hang-ups. Christ came, Christ is here—and so God's love is here. The kingdom is within you and all around you.

How do we live in the tensions we have to face? By living in the kingdom, now. By living the values of that kingdom that Christ taught, even as we await Christ's return. Reach out and grab that kingdom, which is God's gift to us. And every day starts feeling like Christmas.

Six
A Momentum of Joy

Sing aloud, O daughter Zion;
   shout, O Israel!
Rejoice and exult with all your heart,
   O daughter Jerusalem!
The LORD has taken away the judgments against you,
   he has turned away your enemies.
The king of Israel, the LORD, is in your midst;
   you shall fear disaster no more.
On that day it shall be said to Jerusalem:
Do not fear, O Zion;
   do not let your hands grow weak.
The LORD, your God, is in your midst,
   a warrior who gives victory;
he will rejoice over you with gladness,
   he will renew you in his love;
he will exult over you with loud singing
   as on a day of festival. (Zephaniah 3:14–18)

• • • • • • •

I have some help for your next ecclesiastical trivia game: The third Sunday of Advent is called "Guadete Sunday." It's a word that means "rejoice" in Latin. We light the rose-colored candle on the Advent wreath. In some places, the deep purple vestments of Advent, or other church decorations, turn pink as well. In the old days, no musical instruments were played or flowers displayed in the church during Advent, except for this Sunday. The message is pretty clear: lighten up!

Rejoice in the Lord always; again I will say, Rejoice.
Let your gentleness be known to everyone. The Lord is
near. Do not worry about anything, but in everything
by prayer and supplication with thanksgiving let your
requests be made known to God. And the peace of
God, which surpasses all understanding, will guard
your hearts and your minds in Christ Jesus.
(Philippians 4:4–7)

Advent is a season of joyful expectation. We don't go through Advent pretending like we don't know that Jesus will be born. We know the whole story. We know that what we are waiting for has come, so our anticipation is bubbling over in joy. It can't be contained. That's the note that is sounding here. We celebrate the whole mystery, and the dominant response to that mystery is joy.

Julian of Norwich, the great English mystic, had a way of summing up the Christian life. To her, we are meant "to live thankfully and joyfully because of the knowledge of God's love." What a mission statement for Christians. Gratitude and joy are simply the natural responses to all this. If there's not enough gratitude and joy in our lives, maybe that's because there's not enough knowledge of God's love. If people experience their religion as predominantly about fear and guilt and despair, then that religion has nothing to do with the faith of Jesus Christ. That's not why he came. He came that our *"joy may be complete"* (John 15:11).

The prophet Zephaniah says: *"Exult with all your heart, O daughter Jerusalem!"* The Lord is renewing you, restoring you, gathering all the outcasts in. Paul says: *"Rejoice in the Lord always."* Joy has to be always there, always present to us.

So how are we doing with this? Do we "rejoice always"? Is it easy for us to "exult"? Is it easy for us to celebrate, to smile, to enjoy life? To take pleasure in the good things of life?

I have heard that the philosopher Friedrich Nietzsche once spoke in front of a church group. Now, he did not care much for Christians. He looked around the room and said, "Funny, you don't look redeemed." That's sort of funny—but then look at some congregations, and I think we know what he meant. We all have our moods. Emotions are like the tides. They come in and out, they rise and fall. Joy is not a mood. It's not a passing emotion. It's deeper than any current circumstances or feelings we might have. It's a deeper attitude toward reality that makes it easy for us to rejoice, to be thankful, to see the good around us, to take pleasure in what the Lord has done. That joy stays with us regardless of the difficulties we happen to be going through.

Does that sound naive? One reason why some may find it difficult to "shout for joy" is because it feels naive to rejoice. Look at the world we're in and its problems, the wars, the suffering, and pain that runs so deep. Look at the personal crises people have to deal with. Maybe someone is dealing with a health problem. Or a friend is dealing with mental illness, an addiction, or financial troubles. Someone in our family is having problems at school, at work. With all due respect to Zephaniah, not all the lame are healed. Not all the scattered have been gathered.

Is Zephaniah naive? He's actually known as a prophet of doom in the Old Testament. Most of his book is about God's judgment. He lived during the reign of King Josiah. It was a time of corruption. Religiously, the people were turning away from their traditions and worshiping other gods. Politically it was a time of impending war. But it's his book that gives us this passage—one of the most joyful and lively in all the Scriptures.

He gives us this incredible image: *"The LORD, your God, is in your midst...he will rejoice over you with gladness... he will exult over you with loud singing as on a day of festival."* A later verse even depicts God dancing at the festival. God is not only throwing the party here, God is celebrating and singing and dancing with the guests.

Is Paul naive? He's writing to the Philippians from prison. He's writing to friends of his, and he doesn't know if he'll ever see them again. What does he say? *"Rejoice in the Lord always; again I will say, Rejoice."*

Zephaniah and Paul both live in a world of natural disasters, corruption, economic panic, personal crises. They are aware that people set up obstacles to peace, to justice, to their own happiness. They aren't naive. They're not about grinning through the pain or pretending that life is something it isn't. They're rooted in something deeper that went beyond their external circumstances. They are aware that with every obstacle there are greater opportunities, greater possibilities for rejoicing, for bringing joy to others. They see that there is a momentum of joy set up in this world that can't be overcome. The worst that evil can do will not overcome it.

This is the joy that comes to us at Christmastime. It knows in faith that Christ has been born into this world, that Christ is with us now, and that Christ will come again. It's a joy that sees the whole story and knows that it's all in God's hands.

We can be part of that joy. So lighten up!

Seven
Abundance

• • • • • • • •

Remember when we were kids, we'd wait so impatiently for Christmas to come. We wished it would get here faster. Time moved so slowly. As adults, we may have a different experience. We may think of all the things we have to do and wish it would take its time coming.

It's the same objective reality, the same number of hours in the day, but for some it moves too slow, and for some it moves too fast—all based on where we are in life, our experiences, our attitudes.

We see that everywhere. One person may bring an attitude of poverty to everything. No matter how much they get in life, it is never enough; there are always complaints. Another brings an attitude of abundance to everything. No matter what they get in life, it's all seen as a gift. It's more than enough. There is only gratitude. The same objective reality but different experiences, different ways of looking at things.

I worked in a city once where there were two parish churches: one in an affluent part of town, and one in a poor, immigrant area. The affluent church had many programs and resources. Yet the staff always seemed to be complaining about what they didn't have, what they couldn't do. There was always stress and a lack of time. The other church was cramped and the facilities were falling apart; yet they always made do with what they had, and there always seemed to be more room for someone. Things were chaotic at times, but positive energy and laughter filled the hallways. An abundance mentality was at work.

John said to the crowds that came out to be baptized
by him, "You brood of vipers! Who warned you to
flee from the wrath to come? Bear fruits worthy of
repentance. Do not begin to say to yourselves, 'We
have Abraham as our ancestor'; for I tell you, God is
able from these stones to raise up children to Abraham
Even now the ax is lying at the root of the trees; every
tree therefore that does not bear good fruit is cut down
and thrown into the fire."

And the crowds asked him, "What then should we
do?" In reply he said to them, "Whoever has two coats
must share with anyone who has none; and whoever
has food must do likewise." Even tax collectors came
to be baptized, and they asked him, "Teacher, what
should we do?" He said to them, "Collect no more than
the amount prescribed for you." Soldiers also asked
him, "And we, what should we do?" He said to them,
"Do not extort money from anyone by threats or false
accusation, and be satisfied with your wages."
(Luke 3:7-14)

John the Baptist's call to repentance and penance is hardly a
party invitation. Yet it has a positive and practical thrust to it,
one that calls us to the true joy that follows pardon and peace.

Groups of people who had been baptized came to him and
asked what they should do, and he answered: *"Whoever has two
coats must share with anyone who has none."* When we have blessings,
gifts, talents in our lives, we need to share them. When we try to
hoard, we lose. If we move into a fear mentality, we will defeat
ourselves and forget our joy. Share your blessings and you'll find
more blessings, more joy.

Tax collectors came to him. They were despised as collaborators with the Roman occupiers and known as cheats. John tells them: *"Collect no more than the amount prescribed for you."* Soldiers come. He tells them: *"Be satisfied with your wages."* These are people who have power over others. He's basically telling them not to abuse their power. Be content with what is just. Whenever we find that we have power over others—employees, fellow workers, spouses, children, friends, neighbors, strangers—we need to be content with what is just. Act with respect and reverence toward one another, with those God has placed in our lives.

Third Week

These are all practical ways of living in a spirit of gratitude and abundance. At times, we see this. We see that repenting of our pride and acting in simplicity and truth is the simplest thing in the world to do. It's simple because that's the true reality of the world around us: we are surrounded by a gift. We have to go out and do something to avoid that reality. We have to insert pride and dishonesty and fear. We have to create our divisions and nurture our attitude of poverty.

Repentance is actually the realization of seeing things as they truly are. We come to see that our tensions and miseries are of our own making. We come to desire nothing more than to enjoy and cooperate with reality as it is. We begin to see as God sees.

There are those who set up obstacles even to their own happiness, who fundamentally live in an attitude of defeat, of fear, of scarcity in life. And there are those who live out of the victory God brings to life, the victory of God's love in their lives. They can go through the worst in life, and they are still happy with what they have. They live in generosity, abundance, gratitude. All is seen as a gift.

That's one of the messages of this Advent season: You can choose your attitude toward life. You can choose to live in hope and love regardless of the results or lack of results you see. You can act practically, positively, joyfully. Abundantly.

Fourth Week
Mary's Call

Imagine yourself as a living house. God comes in to rebuild that house. At first, perhaps, you can understand what he is doing. He is getting the drains right and stopping the leaks in the roof and so on: you knew that those jobs needed doing and so you are not surprised. But presently He starts knocking the house about in a way that hurts abominably and does not seem to make sense. What on earth is He up to? The explanation is that He is building quite a different house from the one you thought of—throwing out a new wing here, putting on an extra floor there, running up towers, making courtyards. You thought you were going to be made into a decent little cottage: but He is building a palace. He intends to come and live in it himself.

—C. S. LEWIS

One
What About Me?

In the sixth month the angel Gabriel was sent by God to a town in Galilee called Nazareth, to a virgin engaged to a man whose name was Joseph, of the house of David. The virgin's name was Mary. And he came to her and said, "Greetings, favored one! The Lord is with you." But she was much perplexed by his words and pondered what sort of greeting this might be. The angel said to her, "Do not be afraid, Mary, for you have found favor with God. And now, you will conceive in your womb and bear a son, and you will name him Jesus. He will be great, and will be called the Son of the Most High, and the Lord God will give to him the throne of his ancestor David. He will reign over the house of Jacob forever, and of his kingdom there will be no end." Mary said to the angel, "How can this be, since I am a virgin?" The angel said to her, "The Holy Spirit will come upon you, and the power of the Most High will overshadow you; therefore the child to be born will be holy; he will be called Son of God. And now, your relative Elizabeth in her old age has also conceived a son; and this is the sixth month for her who was said to be barren. For nothing will be impossible with God." Then Mary said, "Here am I, the servant of the Lord; let it be with me according to your word." Then the angel departed from her. (Luke 1:26–38)

• • • • • • •

There is a seventeenth-century German mystic named Angelus Silesius. He said, "What does it profit me if Gabriel hails the virgin, unless he brings me the same tidings?"

That's a good question. He is basically asking, "What does all this have to do with us?" There are teachers and preachers who simply spout doctrines without ever getting at that question. That's an adolescent kind of thinking that says this is what you are supposed to believe, so just believe and don't ask any questions. Angelus is different. "What does it profit me?" What does this have to do with me? How does this connect with my life? That's the question that brings us deeper into the story.

Are there areas of our lives where we want to see real change? Do we want healing in our lives? Do we want to overcome fear or isolation or anything that keeps us from living? Do we want to find peace within ourselves, peace with our Creator? Do we want to live in true freedom, with open, hope-filled eyes? Do we want to know the power of love and see that manifested in real ways? Do we want new beginnings, new things happening in our world because of us? Are we ready to believe that nothing is impossible with God? If so, then we had better attend to this story.

This story is about us, and a gentle power that heals us and changes things for the better. It wants to bring us to life. It wants to overflow into our actions. It wants to give birth to Christ in us. The Lord gives us this story to show us how that power works, and to teach us, through Mary, how to respond. Can you think of a place in your life right now where you need that new life, that new birth? Where?

This birth process, like any other, has stages. We see the beginning in this gospel story, the story of an encounter. And within that encounter there are stages, too—levels of understanding and response.

The first stage could be called the stage of "Openness," or "Receptivity." God sends the angel to a little town, Nazareth. Gabriel (in Hebrew, "the power of God") comes to Mary and greets her: *"Greetings, favored one!"* Already this is showing us something: God takes the initiative in this encounter. God sends the messenger to Mary to guide her understanding of how grace is working in her life. She has to listen, be open, be receptive. Can we believe that this is our story, too?

Christianity, like Judaism, is known as a "historical" faith. That is, it is not based merely on a philosophy of life, or on someone's theory or prophecy but on an experience of God acting in human history. Human beings had an *experience*, an experience they came to understand as God's action in history, and therefore as God's revelation. We see it in Israel's experience of liberation from slavery. We see it in the church's experience of Christ's life, death, and resurrection.

Mary sees it in her personal experience. Can we believe in our own experience? Can we believe that God takes the initiative in our lives? God sends an angel. God gives us a new vision, inspires us with new possibilities for our lives. God sets the seed, the desire for a new birth within us. Can we believe that there is a divine spark of life in us, a gentle power at work, and that we can give ourselves over to it?

Another thing about Gabriel's greeting: The angel says, *"The Lord is with you."* This greeting has a pedigree, a powerful significance. Throughout the Bible it presents a challenge. These words are spoken to Isaac, Joshua, Gideon, David:

> The angel of the LORD appeared to him and said to him,
> "The LORD is with you, you mighty warrior."
> (Judges 6:12)

When these words are spoken, they represent an invitation. Someone is being invited to set out from the usual roles they play and to accept a new, crucial role. They are asked to sacrifice, move beyond themselves, to put their trust in God. Moses, at the burning bush, is told the Lord will be with him as he moves out of his comfortable obscurity in order to lead his people out of slavery. Mary is told the Lord is with her as she begins her unique role in the plan of salvation, her journey into unknown risks and possibilities.

Fourth Week

No wonder Mary experiences different emotions in the face of this mystery. We're told she is "perplexed" or "troubled" as she ponders all of this. In the face of a new vision, a new possibility, a new birth for our lives, we can be "troubled." We can feel surprise, confusion—fear of God's call and the change and struggle it entails. We question that vision. We say, "Why me?" We can be blocked by fear when we consider how others will not understand.

Mary wasn't blocked, though. She stays open and receptive. We, too, can't just be open; we have to stay open. This could be called the stage of "Engagement." Mary engages the conversation the angel has begun. She questions. She listens again.

In her engaged receptivity, Mary hears these words: *"Do not be afraid, Mary, for you have found favor with God."* Fear blocks, closes us down, isolates. We tighten up and shrink away. God's favor melts away fear, opens us up, and releases us to trust.

Have we heard those words, those tidings in our own lives? Have we heard that voice that calls us by name and says that you are favored, you are loved? Not because of what you've done or what you haven't done, but because *you are*. God offers his assurance: I made you, I loved you into being. Do not be afraid. You're not going to have to face the challenges of life alone.

You don't have to rely on your abilities alone. My presence, guidance, and protection are with you.

With favor and love comes mission. With that divine spark comes a divine purpose. Mary learns she is called to be part of a movement of God's Spirit that is bigger than herself. She is part of God's purpose for humanity.

Now Mary has to respond again. This is the stage of "Consent." She must respond not with receptivity alone, not with more questions and listening, but with freedom. Her openness becomes active. She did not initiate this encounter or this invitation, but she must choose it. She must say yes, *"let it be. . . ."* Let it happen to me. Let the possibility of new life emerge in me. The Greek word we translate as "let it be," I'm told, does not express passivity, but a joyful desire. She is actively, joyfully saying, "Yes!"

In the same way, we must choose, because that power is a gentle power. It doesn't intrude where it is not wanted. That sweet, divine power doesn't impose its will, but invites us to new life, inviting our participation and cooperation. It invites us to say, "Yes, let it happen to me. I choose that vision."

All of that is just the beginning, the first encounter.

Two
Gestation

• • • • • • •

It begins with "Openness," "Engagement," "Consent." But there are other stages in this birth process. There will be the period of "Gestation." It is a time of waiting, a time of patience. We have to give the newness in us time to develop. We have to carry it to term. We need to be patient with ourselves as we go through a process. We need to foster our trust that new life will come about in God's time.

During Mary's pregnancy, she ponders in her heart what is happening to her; she must guard and nurture the insights and powers she has been given. There are threats to pregnancies, from within and from without. In our eagerness for change, we can get discouraged when it doesn't come fast enough. Doubts and fears return. Judgment or indifference from others takes its toll. Imagine Mary, a young mother, feeling alone, probably rebuked, ridiculed, cursed by those who could never understand her life, her call. How soon the joy of our yes passes. We can feel adrift as the consequences of our decisions confront us. Gestation will demand our active attention and cooperation as we navigate new seas.

One way of cooperating with this gestation period will be to feed ourselves with the truths and personal insights we receive from God's Word. How many times did Mary, in the face of the challenges that threatened her belief, have to remind herself of the words of the angel to her: *"The Lord is with you."* How many times did she have to claim that truth in the face of derision or disregard? She needed to remind herself that in God's plan she was no less one of God's warriors than Gideon or David. This would have renewed her courage and desire to fulfill her call.

What personal insights has the Lord given us to carry us and sustain us? Haven't these become touchstones for us? They may be special prayers, images, or words of Scripture that we return to for solace and renewal, and during our gestation periods, they are like shade in the desert. Or what experiences have we had that remind us of our best selves and our capacity for great-ness? Counselors recommend a discipline for those who may be faced with a challenging task at work or any area of life: in the midst of the anxiety you feel about tackling that task, imagine a time when you were at your strongest. What was it like? How did you act? That is who you are. Part of gestation is calling forth strength and embarking on the tasks that prepare us for even more growth.

Now, Advent waiting is active waiting. Gestation periods have their own opportunities for stepping out with new under-stand and learning, with faith and service to others.

> In those days Mary set out and went with haste to a Judean town in the hill country, where she entered the house of Zechariah and greeted Elizabeth. When Elizabeth heard Mary's greeting, the child leapt in her womb. And Elizabeth was filled with the Holy Spirit and exclaimed with a loud cry, "Blessed are you among women, and blessed is the fruit of your womb. And why has this happened to me, that the mother of my Lord comes to me? For as soon as I heard the sound of your greeting, the child in my womb leapt for joy. And blessed is she who believed that there would be a fulfillment of what was spoken to her by the Lord." (Luke 1:39–45)

Two women with child greet each other, both half scared, half joyful. Elizabeth, blessed by Mary's greeting, feels the child leap in her womb. Mary, perhaps uncertain of what kind of greeting she may receive from her kinswoman, hears words of blessing. "Blessed are you. . . . blessed is the fruit of your womb. . . . *And why has this happened to me, that the mother of my Lord comes to me? . . . Blessed is she who believed."* How sweet those words of blessing must have sounded to Mary's ears. Here, finally, is someone who understands, who does not judge. Here is someone who reverences and honors her for who she is.

Mary's decision to step out in faith and in service to her cousin Elizabeth in her pregnancy shows her active participation in the gestation period. She takes the insights she's been given and puts them into practice. She is vulnerable in relating to others and draws more insights from them. She stays with the process, stays open to the gentle power at work in her. In turn, she receives a blessing that will sustain her for what lies ahead. That's the purpose of gestation: to lead us to a time of completion.

The next stage is "Labor," with its mixture of joy, pain, relief, exhaustion. It's another time of active involvement and cooperation in the birthing process: the need to let go, to relax during early contractions, to endure through pain and the panic of thinking we can't endure, the need to finally bear down.

We become like Mary again. Imagine her, like so many women at that moment of birthing: bearing down with what feels like her last bit of strength. This time, though, she brings forth her own child into the world and into her arms. We, too, need to cultivate that letting go, that trusting endurance, that active involvement, that bearing down with all our strength in giving birth to new life. No matter what stage of life we're in, there's no growth without pain: then comes the joy of embracing that newness within ourselves and encouraging its growth.

Like physical birth, our inner births, our discoveries of divine life within, have a beginning in receptivity and consent; they develop in patience and endurance; and they come to fulfillment in letting go and bearing down. This is a lifelong process, and it brings life to us again and again in God's grace.

This isn't to say the process will always be so clear-cut, well-defined, or predictable. Our stages may be vague or overlapping. There may be times when our receptivity is off, our consent is halfhearted, our endurance is lacking.

But at those times especially, remember Mary. God sends angels to us, too. We can remind ourselves of the Lord's message to her and to each one of us: Do not fear. Your new life is possible and will come, not because of your power, but because of that gentle power that always brings life. The same Spirit who overshadowed a simple woman in Nazareth is at work in us, and promises again: "... *nothing will be impossible with God*" (Luke 1:37).

Three
Blessing and Cursing

· · · · · · ·

O nce I was invited to the home of a friend for dinner with his family. Sometime after dinner, it was time for his little boy, Justin, to go to bed. Justin, about six or seven years old, clearly did not like that idea. He wanted to stay up with everybody else. He started to make every excuse he could, trying to buy some extra time. "Just a few more minutes . . . please!" After he got those, his dad wasn't making any more deals. "My favorite show is on." No. "My teacher said we had to watch it." No. Justin was making his way up the stairs to his bedroom and stopped and called down: "I've got more homework to do." No, you don't. He went up a few more stairs and stopped again. "I need some water." There's water upstairs. Almost to the top of the staircase, he stopped again. "Dad, I want a blessing."

Now, I have to admit that was a new one on me. Apparently, in this house you got blessings. After a moment, his dad laughed. Justin laughed. "Okay, come down for a blessing." Justin ran down the stairs and hopped into his dad's lap with a big grin on his face. My friend laid his hand on the boy's head and said something like, "May the Lord bless you and keep you and make his face shine on you, amen." Justin, satisfied with winning this extra minute, knew his time was up and bounced up the stairs to bed.

Our faith loves blessings. Maybe it's our Jewish roots. We'll bless anything. Like the rabbi in *Fiddler on the Roof* who, when someone asks him if there's a blessing for the czar, says yes: "May God bless and keep the czar...far away from us!"

> But you, O Bethlehem of Ephrathah,
>> who are one of the little clans of Judah,
> from you shall come forth for me
>> one who is to rule in Israel,
> whose origin is from of old,
>> from ancient days. . . .
> And he shall stand and feed his flock in the strength
>> of the LORD,
>> in the majesty of the name of the LORD his God.
> And they shall live secure, for now he shall be great
>> to the ends of the earth;
> and he shall be the one of peace. (Micah 5:2, 4-5)

What exactly is a blessing? We could say it's the opposite of a curse. A curse speaks evil or ill of someone. A blessing speaks well of someone. It speaks goodness on others. In words and gestures we speak praise to God. *"Bless the LORD, O my soul, and do not forget all his benefits"* (Psalm 103:2). We ask God's loving care on us.

We bless everything. People: we pray that God will show love and give help in our daily lives. Places: We give praise for the people who live and work in those places. The prophet Micah blesses Bethlehem. *"But you, O Bethlehem ... from you shall come forth for me one who is to rule ... he shall be the one of peace."* We bless things, and the people who use them. We pray that things will be used for the good of all creation. When a church is blessed at its dedication, there are many signs and symbols used to say that these stones are different. The community of faith who will come here to worship God, who will sing songs in praise to God, who will bless bread and wine in the Lord's memory, makes this place different.

Words and gestures have power. With them we express ourselves to others and to the world. And we are free to use that power. We can use it to curse or tear down, to discourage or divide. Or we can empty them of meaning. We can speak false blessings to mislead, to flatter, or to sell. Think of all the hype we hear at this time of year from those whose only concern is to engage in the commercial side of the holidays. Or we can use words of blessing as a quick fix, to avoid difficulties or responsibilities. St. James asks what good it is to say, *"Go in peace"* (James 2:16) to the neighbor in need without attending to them. An empty gesture.

In the midst of the cursing that goes on in our world, we are called to be a blessing. We are called to bless authentically from our hearts, to use our words and gestures honestly to express our true hopes, and to affirm the goodness around us. We are called to offer blessings graciously, expecting nothing in return, to freely bestow kindness and challenge others in love to be blessings, too. We are called to enjoy and celebrate the goodness of life and to bless the creator and sanctifier of life. We can be a blessing in the midst of the curse.

How will we use our power? I was watching the old, classic version of *The Grapes of Wrath* on television one day. You probably remember it. A poor family that has lost their home travels from Oklahoma to California to look for work. It's a long trek in which they are insulted and taken advantage of repeatedly. In the midst of this, a waitress in a diner sees their plight. The father, with two of his kids, stands at a counter displaying nickel candy. "What can I get for a penny?" he asks. "Two for a penny," she says. She helps him out in his distress, helps him maintain a little dignity. A blessing in the midst of a curse. How many times a day do we have the chance to do something so simple and yet so meaningful?

I read an article once where the author told a story about his "road rage" experience. He had the common experience of a car pulling in front of him in traffic, cutting him off in what seemed to be a careless and arrogant way. It happened at a bad time and the author started to follow the other car in anger. He pulled up in another lane next to the offender, and I'll leave to your imagination the gesture he was preparing to share through his window. But, as he pulled next to the car, he saw a flustered mother with three kids. She noticed him as he glared into the car. Then she held up a sign that read: "I'm sorry!" This was a new one on him, too. Apparently, she'd been in this situation before. Immediately, the tension was broken. He laughed and the anger was gone. He offered a different gesture: a wave with a smile as if to say, "Hope the rest of your day is better." She reminded him that he could easily influence his environment rather than being influenced by it. She offered him a blessing in the midst of an imminent curse.

Will we use our power to bless or to curse? There is a lot of cursing going on. Big ways, little ways. There are millions of refugees in the world, fleeing various conflicts. Like many immigrant groups, they are unwanted much of the time. How often do they feel cursed? How many children grow up in an environment where they feel unwanted? Do you ever read the comments section after an online news article or editorial? It can be shocking to see the ugliness and hatred that is spewed anonymously onto people. If we ourselves are cursed, how tempted are we to respond with a curse, to repay evil with evil? When we're not understood or respected, do we look for a way to lash back? When we see others exploited or hurt, do we pretend not to notice? In all these ways, the world becomes a little more cursed.

Yet, when someone chooses to bless, what a difference it makes. A blessing shines in the darkness. Can you think of a time when you were blessed? Maybe it was receiving an unexpected Christmas card from someone. Or maybe it was an act of kindness that came at the best time. When we know what it is like to receive a blessing, we will start giving blessings. Make this an Advent discipline: when you meet anyone, no matter how small the encounter, say inwardly to yourself, "I want to be a blessing to you." See how that brings to your mind things that you can do to bless others.

We are preparing to celebrate the ultimate blessing we have received. It came first from Bethlehem, from the one *"who shall be the one of peace."* How blessed we are by God, who has taken on every curse. He went to those places of anguish and pain, of feeling alone, abandoned, crying out, *"my God, why have you forsaken me?"*(Matthew 27:46). He went so that we would find his blessing—the blessing of the one who empowers us to bless. The only response to that Good News is to bless and bless again. Even if someone answers with a curse, it changes nothing. We bless again.

As we journey through Advent, even if blessings seem few, choose to exercise your spiritual power to bless: by showing understanding, by caring and praying, by using words and gestures that express the love that the Lord has put into us. Take no one for granted. Bless a child, your family, the strangers you meet. A blessing will return. In these days, there is time to receive blessings and to bless again.

Four

Pregnant Hope

Now the birth of Jesus the Messiah took place in this way. When his mother Mary had been engaged to Joseph, but before they lived together, she was found to be with child from the Holy Spirit. Her husband Joseph, being a righteous man and unwilling to expose her to public disgrace, planned to dismiss her quietly. But just when he had resolved to do this, an angel of the Lord appeared to him in a dream and said, "Joseph, son of David, do not be afraid to take Mary as your wife, for the child conceived in her is from the Holy Spirit. She will bear a son, and you are to name him Jesus, for he

will save his people from their sins."
(Matthew 1:18-21)

. . . .

God sends signs: dreams, images, prophetic words. We
send signs to one another during this season, too: images,
messages, Christmas cards, Christmas e-mails, party invitations.
As the world gets darker and colder for so many, we send
greetings of hope. In the dark of winter, we send warm words
and string up bright lights.

I enjoy receiving all kinds of cards and images: a dove of
peace, angels singing, Donner and Blitzen. But most of the
images tend to be of a mother and child. They are traditional
images, Renaissance, Byzantine icons, contemporary, African,
Asian. Something about that image crosses all barriers.

I came across a devotion to Mary that I was unfamiliar with.
I was living in Washington, DC, and visited a church served by
Dominican friars. There was a small statue there of Mary about
six months pregnant. Apparently, there is a Dominican devotion
to Mary as a pregnant woman. It's not an image we're used to
(even if the common figure of Our Lady of Guadalupe is said to
be a portrait of the pregnant Mary). We might even be taken
aback if we were to receive a Christmas card of a very pregnant
Mary. Yet this seems like a very appropriate Advent devotional
image. The image of expectant parents awaiting the birth of
their child is a good one to express the hope and anticipation
of the season.

Not long after that, I decided to learn more about pregnancy.
With no firsthand experience to go on, I decided I would call
my sister-in-law Barbara. I asked what it was like to be pregnant
with my nephew Benjamin.

Barbara wasn't put off by the question at all. She talked about an experience of nurturing. Nurturing her baby with her body. She became aware of wanting to eat the right things. "No more diet sodas," she said. "Don't even mention wine to me." But it went beyond food and drink. She wanted to nurture the baby with her thoughts. As she felt her body changing, her thoughts became more directed to her baby. She felt she was nurturing him with thoughts and plans, dreams and prayer.

Fourth
Week

She spoke of her pregnancy as a hopeful time. She described what seemed not so much like kicks as a "fluttering." The stirring of life within. It was exciting and wonderful. She thought, "It's really happening. The baby is here." That reminded me of a woman in an office I worked in once. She would introduce her soon-to-be-born child to people when they came in. "This is Christopher," she'd say.

Barbara also felt a sense of connection during her pregnancy. She felt linked to the past. She thought of her own mother and all the other women who had gone through what she was going through. She thought of Mary. She also felt linked to the future. She thought about her own family. She thought about what she would take from her parents and what she would change in forming her own family.

Barbara spoke of the patience required in her pregnancy, especially toward the end. She would say to herself, "Come on...I want to see you!" Then she would remember that she would just have to let things happen. Like Mary's *"let it be."* She had to continue to let this be a gentle time of waiting. The picture I was getting was of a hopeful, patient, nurturing time.

But that wasn't all. There was another side to pregnancy she spoke of. There was occasional worry and anxiety. She wondered: Will the baby be okay? How will all this come out? (And *literally*, how will all this come out?) Going through this for the first time, not knowing what to expect from labor, there was the fear of the unknown. Once I heard a comedian talking about her anxiety about labor. She mentioned how her own mother was in labor for thirty-six hours. She followed that with: "I don't want to do anything I enjoy for thirty-six hours!"

Barbara talked about fear. She wondered at times if she was doing the right thing, considering the world we live in, and what can make this world a frightening place. Should we be bringing another child into the world? Will we be able to provide safety? Will we be able to give our child what's best? There was another picture emerging: one of doubt, uncertainty, risk.

> Again the LORD spoke to Ahaz, saying, Ask a sign of the LORD your God; let it be deep as Sheol or high as heaven. But Ahaz said, I will not ask, and I will not put the LORD to the test. Then Isaiah said: "Hear then, O house of David! Is it too little for you to weary mortals, that you weary my God also? Therefore the Lord himself will give you a sign. Look, the young woman is with child and shall bear a son, and shall name him Immanuel." (Isaiah 7:10–14)

Ahaz has doubts. Judah is in a period of national doubt. The powerful northern kingdom of Syria is threatening to march on Jerusalem. Things are getting cold and dark. And Isaiah sends the king a sign: A woman with child. And the name of the child is Immanuel, "God is with us."

No matter how bad things look, no matter how bad things get—"Immanuel."

In the Gospel, Mary knows uncertainty. She's already given her "fiat." She's already said yes to God. Let it be done. She said yes, not knowing all that affirmation could entail. Will she have to go through it alone? Will Joseph be strong enough to say yes, too? Will he be able to endure the struggles of a pregnancy that breaks the rules? Or will he put her aside? Quietly get rid of her?

We keep looking for a way out. God keeps offering a way in: opening doors, inviting us into the mystery. When we want a way out of responsibility, God offers guidance. We want an easy way out of problems, and God offers support and growth through the struggle. We want a way out of mystery, we want simple answers, and God offers a deeper clarity. God sets us on a path of trust.

> When Joseph awoke from sleep, he did as the angel of the Lord commanded him; he took her as his wife. (Matthew 1:24)

Mary and Joseph both struggle to understand. "How can this be?" But they keep listening. Then comes a time for Joseph's fiat. Here is a man of faith who can perceive signs, dreams: "*Joseph, son of David, do not be afraid.*" The Holy Spirit is with this child. Name him Jesus.

All around us there are powerful threats to our hope, great uncertainties in our lives. We need signs of hope. Expectant parents become signs of hope in the midst of doubt, patience in the midst of uncertainty. For Barbara, the sign was that fluttering, from a source not yet seen. It was the promise of new life. Her child was a sign of hope. And thinking about Mary and her child made a difference to her.

There was a Dominican mystic of the Middle Ages named Meister Eckhart. Maybe he knew this devotion to the pregnant Mary. Maybe that prompted him to speak about the birth of God in our souls. He talked about Christians not only as children of God, but also as mothers of God. He asked: What are we pregnant with? What are we patiently nurturing within us? What thoughts, dreams, plans, prayers? What do we give birth to in our words and actions and creativity? Are we pregnant with the same hope and grace that Mary literally was pregnant with and gave birth to?

We have been given a sign: Mary heavy with child, a child who, even before he's born, is bringing reconciliation to others, healing his family, bringing more hope to the world. That message is still being sent. That sign is still being given. It's Immanuel: God with us. God reaching out to us, ready to be welcomed within. Ready to be born.

Five
Oil of Gladness

The spirit of the LORD GOD is upon me,
    because the LORD has anointed me;
he has sent me to bring good news to the oppressed,
    to bind up the brokenhearted,
to proclaim liberty to the captives,
    and release to the prisoners;
to proclaim the year of the LORD's favor,
    and the day of vengeance of our God;
    to comfort all who mourn;

to provide for those who mourn in Zion—
　　to give them a garland instead of ashes,
the oil of gladness instead of mourning,
　　the mantle of praise instead of a faint spirit.
(Isaiah 61:1-3)

* * * * * * *

We know the word *Christ* in Greek means the "anointed one." And so we think of the word of the prophet Isaiah: *"The spirit of the LORD GOD is upon me, because the LORD has anointed me."*

The Spirit anointed Jesus for his role, his mission as the Messiah. This is God's initiative, and only God can accomplish that saving role. To know who we are as Christians, as his followers, is to know that we are anointed, too. We are anointed by the same Spirit to be like him, to prepare Christ's way. We are called to make him easier to find: in our words and actions, in our presence in the world.

What is that going to look like? It's going to look like Jesus. We'll learn how to *"bind up the brokenhearted."* We won't be a source of harm to others, but a healing presence in the world. We'll learn how to bring *"liberty to the captives."* We'll take the gifts we've been given—intellectual, physical, emotional—and we'll develop them for service. We'll *"bring good news to the oppressed"* to those in need.

We're anointed to bring Good News to others. When people see us coming, will they say, "Here comes good news!" Or will they say, "Here comes bad news"? Think of different people in our lives. When they show up, we already know what's coming. Who will we be for others? To become Good News, we need to receive Good News. We need to taste it. We need feed on what is truly human. We need to feed on the words of Scripture, the truths of faith, the message of God's love, the Eucharist—and we'll learn how to be Good News for others.

> And we urge you, beloved, to admonish the idlers, encourage the fainthearted, help the weak, be patient with all of them. See that none of you repays evil for evil, but always seek to do good to one another and to all. Rejoice always, pray without ceasing, give thanks in all circumstances; for this is the will of God in Christ Jesus for you. (1 Thessalonians 5:14-18)

To bring Good News to others, we need to develop more fully those spiritual disciplines that St. Paul speaks of: the ability to *"rejoice always, pray without ceasing, give thanks in all circumstances."* We've received a gift. Simply recognize it, rejoice in it, and be thankful for it — and that thankfulness will have its effects. Our life activity becomes a prayer.

One effect of this thankfulness and rejoicing will be the gift of perspective. Sometimes the smallest things can get us down, ruin our day. When we keep rejoicing, we keep our perspective. There are four words that will help us to do that. You've heard them before: "this too shall pass."

The author Og Mandino, in his book *The Greatest Salesman in the World* proposes these words as a spiritual discipline.[5] Repeat them in every circumstance, he says, and they will carry you through every adversity, for there are no truer words. When your heart is breaking, say them and you'll be consoled. When you've been offended and are dealing with hurt and anger, say them and you won't overreact. In the face of failure or success, say them and you'll keep your balance, your feet on the ground. When you're stressed or overly serious, say them and you'll find humor in everything. Human beings are never so comical as when we take ourselves too seriously.

"This too shall pass." The petty little things that burden us today — what will they mean ten years from now? A thousand years from now? The candles of the Advent wreath carry multiple meanings. One thought is that each candle represents a thousand years of waiting for the Messiah. That's perspective.

*Fourth
Week*

Another effect of rejoicing in our lives will be action. Rejoicing gives us energy. We act from that true place at our center, beneath the swirl of emotion, beyond the hurts or rejection we may have experienced. We act from that childlike place of trust, wonder, and freedom within. Great things emerge from our center. Joy and creative action rise together from our center.

I think of a medical doctor I met once at a conference. He told me that in the neighborhood where he worked there were no services for homeless mentally ill people. He thought to himself, "What is the church doing?" And then it clicked for him: "I am the church." And so he got started.

I think of Mary Agee, who started what's called "The Nurturing Network." She was a business executive working in high-powered companies in Manhattan, who saw young mothers in crisis pregnancies with nowhere to go. So she simply started reaching out one by one, gathering others who wanted to help. Her efforts resulted in an international network of assistance with tens of thousands of volunteers. Look at her story and you see joy in action.

What story are we writing? We often forget the gift. Difficulties hit us. Friends give up on us. We find ourselves wallowing in familiar miseries. We're too tired to act. Is our story one in which we rejoice often or seldom?

This is when the "discipline" comes in. Go back to the center. Remind yourself of all that passes. Pray in gratitude for all that has been given. Some psychologists recommend keeping a gratitude journal: simply write down the things that happened that day for which you are grateful. Write five things as a discipline. You won't notice anything at first. But over time, a new perspective and contentment will grow. St. Paul was recommending this from the beginning of the church. Everything, every small gift, every small trial, was seen in light of the great gift that could never be taken away.

We, too, can ground ourselves in that gift that is greater than us. Every discipline, every choice, every action can be rooted there. And we will find *"a garland instead of ashes, the oil of gladness instead of mourning, the mantle of praise instead of a faint spirit."*

Six
Sympathy

· · · · · · ·

One can easily see the Greek root *pathos* in the word *sympathy*. It relates to feeling, emotion, experience. When we sympathize with others, we are aware of their feelings and understand their experience, and we are concerned for their well-being. Most likely we think of sympathizing with another's sorrow.

I'm told that in the German language there are two words for our idea of sympathy. One form expresses sympathy for another's sorrow. Another form expresses sympathy with another's joy. It's used when one is happy for another and rejoicing with them.

I wonder if it is harder for us ordinarily to express this second type of sympathy. When we see someone in trouble or pain, we may feel more ready to express our sympathy. But when someone is doing great, perhaps much better than we are, other feelings may arise in us more readily: envy, jealousy, or frustration with our own lot. That may certainly get in the way of our rejoicing with them.

To be "sympathetic" in this way, to show our care for another in whatever circumstances they are in, flows from a certain contact with reality and a basic contentment within ourselves that allows us to empathize with both pain and joy. It contrasts significantly with the competition and falsehood we are often caught up in.

In the Scriptures, we find people rejoicing all the time. The community rejoices with Elizabeth:

> Now the time came for Elizabeth to give birth, and she bore a son. Her neighbors and relatives heard that the Lord had shown his great mercy to her, and they rejoiced with her. (Luke 1:57-58)

And as we've seen, Elizabeth rejoices with Mary. Even John the Baptist, as a child in the womb, gets into the act:

> When Elizabeth heard Mary's greeting, the child leapt in her womb. And Elizabeth was filled with the Holy Spirit and exclaimed with a loud cry, "Blessed are you among women, and blessed is the fruit of your womb." (Luke 1:41-42)

We saw also how the prophet Zephaniah depicts God rejoicing over the people of Israel, to the point of throwing a wild, heavenly party for them:

The LORD, your God, is in your midst,
    a warrior who gives victory. . . .
he will exult over you with loud singing
    as on a day of festival. (Zephaniah 3:17–18)

The name Immanuel is most associated with the Messiah at this time of year. "God with us." How evocative a concept when we consider our capacity to sympathize. God is with us, not only in our pain and sorrow and need, but also in our joy. In the scriptural story, God is the one who brings our joy, shares it, and enlivens it. Ultimately, that's the source of the deeper contentment that allows us to sympathize with others regardless of our circumstances or theirs. We share burdens and joys together. We carry them and celebrate them together.

The voice of my beloved!
    Look, he comes,
leaping upon the mountains,
    bounding over the hills.
My beloved is like a gazelle
    or a young stag.
Look, there he stands
    behind our wall,
gazing in at the windows,
    looking through the lattice.
My beloved speaks and says to me:
"Arise, my love, my fair one,
    and come away;
for now the winter is past,
    the rain is over and gone.
The flowers appear on the earth;

the time of singing has come,
and the voice of the turtledove
    is heard in our land.
The fig tree puts forth its figs,
    and the vines are in blossom;
    they give forth fragrance.
Arise, my love, my fair one,
    and come away.
O my dove, in the clefts of the rock,
    in the covert of the cliff,
let me see your face,
    let me hear your voice;
for your voice is sweet,
    and your face is lovely. (Song of Solomon 2:8–14)

*Fourth
Week*

It's interesting that in this last week before Christmas, this passage from the Old Testament book Song of Solomon appears in the weekday liturgical readings. In the Northern Hemisphere, these are the days leading up to the winter solstice, the darkest time of the year. *"For now the winter is past … the flowers appear."* As we get our first taste of winter, we're told: spring is coming!

For us, it can be another kind of reminder: that when things seem their darkest, when our circumstances seem bleakest, a deeper kind of springtime is not only coming, but is already here, at work in us. When we meet those who are most in need, those who are struggling through the darkest winter, we sympathize with their pain. In our concern and care for them, we bring them what we can of that springtime. When we meet those who are finding new life, who are experiencing gifts and promises fulfilled, we sympathize with their joy. We raise our voices with them and toast the goodness they receive.

In both instances, there is springtime: an awakening we come to know in the encounter with the beloved who is searching us out. It is the springtime of life and love that appears whenever it will and can be celebrated whenever we wish. It is beginning to flower, *"bounding over the hills,"* *"looking through the lattice,"* as we ready ourselves for the birth of a Savior.

Seven
Newness

Now the time came for Elizabeth to give birth, and she bore a son. Her neighbors and relatives heard that the Lord had shown his great mercy to her, and they rejoiced with her.

On the eighth day they came to circumcise the child, and they were going to name him Zechariah after his father. But his mother said, "No; he is to be called John." They said to her, "None of your relatives has this name." (Luke 1:57–61)

• • • • • • •

In some cultures, there are rules about the naming of children. In my own Italian-American milieu, there was once a strict ordering involved: the first boy was named after the grandfather on the father's side, the second boy after the father. I noticed once in an old scrapbook that I was not named until two days after my birthday and that my name did not follow the rules. My middle name is the same as my father's, but my first seemed to come out of the blue. I never really got a full explanation for this.

Naming a child represents both continuity and discontinuity. A child is born into a tradition, a history that is handed on to him or her. A name given to that child from that tradition, from the loving relationships that helped to form a family, is a beautiful way to recognize that heritage as something living and growing. And yet, every child is a mystery, a new and unrepeatable event. The world has never seen anything like this before and will be forever changed because of it. That newness also has to be recognized.

Elizabeth and Zechariah, John the Baptist's parents, as well as Mary and Joseph, represent the faithful people of the covenant, that unique relationship with God handed on to the people of Israel. They provide the tradition, heritage, and soil for new life to grow. There is continuity here. Yet both John and Jesus are named by angels. There is discontinuity, too. God's people are being prepared for a new act in their history. God brought them this far, speaking through prophets, but now God will speak in a new way. John will be the herald of this newness; Jesus will be the revealer of it.

> Then his father Zechariah was filled with the Holy Spirit and spoke this prophecy:
> "Blessed be the Lord God of Israel,
>   for he has looked favorably on his people and redeemed them.
> He has raised up a mighty savior for us
>   in the house of his servant David...." (Luke 1:67–69)

Every parent, holding their child for the first time, recognizes the gift and the hope that has been given to them. Some glimpse the Lord's hand at work, God's mysterious plan encompassing them. God's initiative always calls forth our response. For Zechariah, the response is first a song of praise. The same is true of Mary's canticle in Luke's Gospel, her famous "Magnificat" (the name comes from the first word in the Latin version of the song):

> And Mary said,
> "My soul magnifies the Lord,
>   and my spirit rejoices in God my Savior,
> for he has looked with favor on the lowliness of his
> servant.
>   Surely, from now on all generations will call me
> blessed;
> for the Mighty One has done great things for me,
>   and holy is his name.
> His mercy is for those who fear him
>   from generation to generation.
> He has shown strength with his arm;
>   he has scattered the proud in the thoughts of their
> hearts.
> He has brought down the powerful from their
> thrones,
>   and lifted up the lowly;
> he has filled the hungry with good things,
>   and sent the rich away empty.
> He has helped his servant Israel,
>   in remembrance of his mercy,
> according to the promise he made to our ancestors,
>   to Abraham and to his descendants forever."
> (Luke 1:46–55)

Both Zechariah and Mary celebrate the continuity of God's gifts in the people's history as well as the discontinuity of God's definitive actions that are now coming to pass. Both sing in awe before the hope that is dawning on them.

There are many places in our lives where we see the intertwining of continuity and discontinuity, of history and newness. We take the best from our tradition and then we strike out on our own. Think of something as small as a young family trying to figure out its own Christmas traditions: They want to pass on those things that gave them such good memories, while they also try to create ways to celebrate their new reality. Think of something as large as people organizing to work for justice and to spread peace. They may be inspired by great saints or prophetic figures from the past, while they also try to bring that spirit to issues and problems of the present.

> See, I am sending my messenger to prepare the way before me, and the Lord whom you seek will suddenly come to his temple. The messenger of the covenant in whom you delight—indeed, he is coming, says the LORD of hosts. (Malachi 3:1)

This Christmas we will receive a gift that is both old and new. Something is being passed on to us, and something is being called out of us. It is a mystery, Mary tells us, which shakes the world out of its complacency and invites our participation. God's initiative calls for our response. There is a continuity with the ancient covenant that was spoken at the creation of the world and at Mount Sinai, and now it is being spoken for you. It gives you a name, deep in your soul, your "temple." It is coming to be born for you.

The Feast

Christmas
Week

And when we give each other Christmas gifts in his
name, let us remember that he has given us sun, moon,
stars, earth with all its forests and oceans and all that
lives and moves upon them. He has given us all green
things and everything that blossoms and bears fruit —
and all that we have misused — and to save us from
our own foolishness, he came down to earth and gave
us himself.

—SIGRID UNDSET

One
Sacred Places, Sacred Times

The people who walked in darkness
    have seen a great light;
those who lived in a land of deep darkness—
    on them light has shined. (Isaiah 9:2)

• • • • • • • •

Certain places in the world seem to have a special quality to them. They are mystical, powerful. People notice that and return to them. The first time I visited northern New Mexico I felt that way. There was something about the landscape, being in the midst of those canyons. It can make one feel small and open up a different way of seeing, a different reality. I've heard people talk about places in Ireland that way or the Holy Land. Maybe Yosemite has done that for you. Or maybe there is a special church or shrine that you like to visit. Maybe you have your own special place, a personal spot that you return to because of its personal significance.

These places bring us out of the ordinary to see in a new way, to see what is most real. The effect is that, hopefully, when we return to our ordinary environment some of that mystery and wonder remains. We appreciate our home and our ordinary lives in a new way.

That's not just true of places. There are special times, too. There are times of our lives or times of the year that are like that. This is one of them. People who celebrate Christmas, and even people who don't, notice it. They notice there's a different quality in the air leading up to Christmas.

People seem different. People are more willing to open up. They open up their calendars to schedule times for celebration. They open up their address books to send greetings, messages, gifts, or blessings. They open their homes to receive gifts. And, yes, they open their checkbooks, more willing to give alms, to remember those in need.

The Feast

They open their hearts to each other in new ways, as well. They're more open to relating, to forgiving, to remembering. They put up lights, and light candles in the darkness.

Special places and times are not special because they offer a break from reality, an escape from the ordinary, dreary, mundane. Times and places are special, sacred, set apart, because they tell us the truth. They tell us what is always and everywhere true.

We need them, because if we didn't have them, we'd forget. We'd lose our connection with that truth. We'd start living a lie, or we'd really start living in the dreariness. We need this sacred time, and God provides it.

There's a story that you may have heard, since it's well known, a true story from the First World War. In fact, a movie was made about it called *Joyeux Noel*. Here's one person's account of it:

Something occurred on December 24, 1914. It happened near Flanders in Belgium on a battlefield of the First World War. The story is told by Peter Gouge, a British soldier who was standing guard that night.

All of a sudden from the German lines the sounds of a Christmas carol came drifting across the battlefield. Silent Night. He started to sing. Others started to sing. The whole British line started singing in English.

The Germans responded with a German carol. Back and forth, it continued until just before dawn when a glimmer of light moved out of the German lines towards the British. One of their soldiers was picking his way across no-man's land holding aloft a small tree decorated with flickering candles. He reached the barbed wire, and leaned over and said in English "Merry Christmas."

As dawn broke, soldiers on both sides emerged from the trenches, shook hands, embraced, exchanged cigarettes and chocolates. A truce was declared to bury the dead on each side. One German gave a British soldier a letter to his English girlfriend.

Upon hearing of this lapse in discipline, this unauthorized truce, the generals on both sides transferred these troops and replaced them. On December 26th the killing resumed.

There are times and places that are so sacred, that even when we try to block out their light through our human faults and limitations, that light still breaks through. A deeper truth and love breaks through and it is seen. But the point for us is that it's not meant to be over on the 26th. Our hope is to take it with us. Not superficially, but to let that deeper truth make a difference that lasts.

In that region there were shepherds living in the fields, keeping watch over their flock by night. Then an angel of the Lord stood before them, and the glory of the Lord shone around them, and they were terrified. But the angel said to them, "Do not be afraid; for see—I am bringing you good news of great joy for all the people:

to you is born this day in the city of David a Savior, who
is the Messiah, the Lord. This will be a sign for you: you
will find a child wrapped in bands of cloth and lying
in a manger." And suddenly there was with the angel
a multitude of the heavenly host, praising God and
saying,

"Glory to God in the highest heaven,
and on earth peace among those whom he favors!"
(Luke 2:8–14)

*The
Feast*

Shepherds are earthy, down-to-earth folks. Living with the
sheep, living in the fields, sleeping on the ground. They're
nobodies. But they're watching, waiting, ready.

A light breaks through to them. Angels start singing,
announcing: This is the time! God is acting in human history.
God does not leave us in our human tragedy, our sin, our
failings. God does not abandon us in our pain, questions, hope.
God comes to redeem us. A Savior is born. Heaven and earth
are uniting.

And these shepherds get it. They understand. They aren't nobodies. They aren't outcasts. God comes to everyone. God comes
to them, welcomes them, heals them. Nothing can be the same.

This most sacred time in human history returns to us today
and tells us what is always, everywhere true. It tells us that our
time, our place is sacred. It tells us that God reaches out to us
in Jesus, offering hope, healing our hearts, teaching us to reach
out to one another.

Is there any wonder why early Christians chose the time of
the winter solstice, the darkest time of year in the northern
hemisphere, the time when the days are shortest, to celebrate
Christ's birth? This is the time of year when a subtle shift

happens. Little by little, each day, the daylight returns. Light begins to overcome darkness. The poetry of the cosmos is telling the same story. But it's not easy to recognize at first. The weight of the darkness, the dreariness, is strong. To perceive the shift, you have to be like the shepherds: gazing, taking time to watch, waiting for the Lord's revelation.

We don't have to work so hard to see the darkness. Maybe it's the personal darkness of fear, doubt, illness, or addiction. Maybe it's the emotional, relational, or financial challenges that continue to weigh on us. Maybe it's the darkness of sin in the world, the weight of human destructiveness enveloping our consciousness.

In the days leading up to Christmas 2012, the residents of Newtown, Connecticut, began taking down their Christmas lights and decorations. After a horrific attack by a gunman on children and teachers in a local school, it was understandable. They had to observe their grief. Yet, on Christmas Eve, it was reported that in neighborhoods throughout the town, many homes were putting lights up again, but not the same ones. People put twenty-six luminarias, for the twenty-six victims who were slain, in their front yards. This was a different way to support one another at a sacred time. People who walked in darkness had seen a great light.

Why is this time, this place set apart? How is it special? What do we remember this day? Christmas tells us: light, divine light, has broken through to the world in Jesus, who, in John's Gospel, says, "*I am the light of the world.*" My teaching, my words, my actions, my example, my love, my sacrifice: these are what will show you the way out of darkness and into the light.

What time in your life is this? Where are you sitting? It is a special time, a sacred place. It is set apart to tell you what is always, everywhere true. The sky is illuminated. Angels are singing. Here and now. They sing as we watch a child open a present, or as we gather with a family for dinner. They sing in a good deed done, a spark of insight that moves us, or in our awareness of God's mercy in prayer.

The Feast

Always and everywhere—the mystery and wonder of God is present, a God who unites heaven and earth to reach us, to reveal his love, to pull us into his kingdom of light.

Two
Ready to Be Found

· · · · · · ·

Here's an old Sunday school joke: A teacher begins her religious education class with a question to her students: "Where do you find Christ?" She gives them a little time to think, then points to one of them, then another, and another. To her surprise, they're actually coming up with some encouraging answers. Then she notices a boy in back who's been in his own world, not paying much attention. So she says, "What about you? Where do you find Christ?" He's still in his own dreamland. Now she's standing over his desk. "Excuse me..." Suddenly he's awake: "Who, me?" "Yeah, you. Where do you find Jesus?" He answers... *drum roll*... "Why, is he lost?"

I once heard a preacher build a whole sermon around that joke. How does Jesus get lost? Sometimes we're caught up in all the chaos of life. We go about with all the activity and shopping and preparations for Christmas. We get through the parties, the expectations, the necessities. And it feels like Christ is nowhere to be found. Have we been paying attention?

I heard a college student I know say, "I feel like a gerbil running around in one of those wheels." It was his way of saying, "I'm doing all these things, but I'm not reflecting on my experience. I'm not paying attention to why I'm doing it, or where I'm going, or what's most important." It's easy to miss that, to lose our bearings.

Think of some of the secular perks that we consume, and that make us feel part of the trendy rush of life: Starbucks, yoga class, Netflix, or, of course, your latest phone. We're accustomed to them, and we certainly enjoy them. But they're not enough. How many people, after achieving all the things we're told are important — the title, salary, right house and neighborhood, all the things we're told we need to possess to "make it" — then ask themselves, "Is that all there is?" All that isn't enough. Our souls need more.

We go through all kinds of crises: political, institutional, financial, personal, family. There are times when we realize that we're missing something. We've lost something. That's when we have to go looking for it, searching for it.

Where do we find Christ? The message of the Scriptures is that Christ wants to be found. Christ is ready to be found.

For Zion's sake I will not keep silent,
    and for Jerusalem's sake I will not rest,
until her vindication shines out like the dawn,
    and her salvation like a burning torch. . . .
You shall be a crown of beauty in the hand of the LORD,
    and a royal diadem in the hand of your God.
You shall no more be termed Forsaken,
    and your land shall no more be termed Desolate;
but you shall be called My Delight Is in Her,

and your land Married;
for the LORD delights in you,
    and your land shall be married.
For as a young man marries a young woman,
    so shall your builder marry you,
and as the bridegroom rejoices over the bride,
    so shall your God rejoice over you. (Isaiah 62:1, 3-5)

Isaiah the prophet says, *"the LORD delights in you."* It's like a bridegroom rejoicing in his bride. This is the image he gives us: it is like lovers who've found each other. They run to embrace each other. Isaiah also uses the image of a sentinel running to bring good news: *"How beautiful upon the mountains are the feet of the messenger who announces peace, who brings good news"* (Isaiah 52:7).

These are some of the images that are supposed to hint at what it's like to find God's presence, God's purpose in our lives.

God wants to embrace you. Not once, but throughout your days. God is ready to meet you. Just to hear that makes us readier to find him.

> Joseph also went from the town of Nazareth in Galilee to Judea, to the city of David called Bethlehem, because he was descended from the house and family of David. He went to be registered with Mary, to whom he was engaged and who was expecting a child. While they were there, the time came for her to deliver her child. And she gave birth to her firstborn son and wrapped him in bands of cloth, and laid him in a manger, because there was no place for them in the inn.
>
> In that region there were shepherds living in the fields, keeping watch over their flock by night. Then an angel

of the Lord stood before them, and the glory of the Lord
shone around them. . . . (Luke 2:4-9)

St. Luke, in his version of the Christmas story, begins with
shepherds. They are the first to receive the Good News.

Why shepherds? They're in the background. No one thinks of
them out in the fields. But we're told they have certain qualities.
They're "watchful," they have to keep watch over their flocks.
They have to be ready to swing into action to protect them.
They pay attention.

To those who are watchful, angels appear. They will bring
news of something that can change everything, something that
brings the healing, love, and meaning you've been looking for.
They speak. They sing. They point to a reality that is born into
the world today. The Savior is born. So get up! Go out and find
him, because he wants to be found.

Sometimes we have to be like the shepherds. We have to pay
attention. We have to listen. We have to be watchful to find
Christ, to see how Christ wants to break into our lives. Sometimes we have to be like the angels who point to Christ. We
have to bring Christ's message of love to others. We have to
celebrate and sing about what Christ has done for us.

St. John of the Cross, the Spanish mystic, once said, "Where
there is no love, put love, and you will find love." We could say,
"When you're looking for Christ, bring Christ, and you will find
Christ." Find Christ's love within you and bring it to others.
Suddenly Christ is everywhere.

"Where do you find Christ?" the teacher asked. The girl
answered, "After I get up in the morning and before I go down
to breakfast, before all the craziness of the day begins, I pray
for a few moments in the quiet. I find Christ there." Then the

teacher points to another one: "Where do you find Christ?" The boy answers, "When I see people giving to others who are in need, knowing that they can't give anything back, but just because they're generous and loving, that's where I find Christ." Another says, "At the dinner we have on Christmas Day when all our family and friends get together and we eat and play games and laugh all night, because it's Jesus' birthday." Not so tough a question after all.

I came across a quote from St. Thérèse of Lisieux: "The God who comes to us as an infant can only be mercy and love." Every time we look at a Nativity scene, God reveals mercy and love. What happened on Christmas only shows us mercy and love.

This is the time to remember all of that. We remember how our God rejoices and delights in us. So much so that he didn't want to remain hidden. God didn't want to leave us alone in the struggles and doubts and questions of life. God came to us in person, in flesh and blood, to be found.

The Feast

Three
Singing

In the beginning was the Word,
and the Word was with God,
and the Word was God.
He was in the beginning with God.
All things came into being through him,
and without him not one thing came into being.
What has come into being in him was life,

and the life was the light of all people.
The light shines in the darkness,
and the darkness did not overcome it. (John 1:1–5)

* * * * * * * *

The picture we paint of the Nativity in our imaginations
is usually so comforting. The manger, the angels, the
shepherds—all the earthy and heavenly details we love—call
to mind the warm feelings and thoughts we associate with this
time of year.

The liturgies of Christmas don't waste any time, however,
leaving those Matthean and Lukan images behind. The liturgy
turns quickly to the prologue of St. John's Gospel as an essential
Christmas text. Here we have a different take on the Nativity
story. This version isn't interested in earthy details. It's interested in what it all *means*. And so John turns to poetry, theology,
signs, and symbols.

T. S. Eliot spoke of poetry's "raid on the inarticulate." Some
would say that John's prologue represents an early Christian
hymn (with some commentary interspersed throughout). This
is a mystery that goes beyond prose. To reflect on this mystery
we need music; we need to sing. That's how one approaches
a mystery that is so transcendent, yet so close. We may miss
the swaddling clothes, the animals, and the guiding star, but
this story is always told against the background of eternity. One
bows before this mystery. One sings.

Like any love song, John gropes for words to convey an
experience of wonder and healing that seems to defy articulation.
Yet at the heart of the mystery that we bow before, the lyrics
ring out:

There was a man sent from God, whose name was
John. He came as a witness to testify to the light, so
that all might believe through him. He himself was not
the light, but he came to testify to the light. The true
light, which enlightens everyone, was coming into the
world.

He was in the world, and the world came into being
through him; yet the world did not know him. He came
to what was his own, and his own people did not
accept him. But to all who received him, who believed
in his name, he gave power to become children of God,
who were born, not of blood or of the will of the flesh
or of the will of man, but of God.

And the Word became flesh
and lived among us,
and we have seen his glory,
the glory as of a father's only son,
full of grace and truth. (John 1:6–14)

Our words are extensions of ourselves into our world and to
the "other." When we speak, we take a risk. Our words, like our
children, take on a life of their own, for better or for worse,
when received by others.

God's Word is God's capacity for self-expression and
revelation. Just as in the beginning it comes to create, so it
comes in new and marvelous ways to redeem, to raise up, to
renew creation. Here, John says, is God's self-expression in a
most unique way: the Word comes, like the relationship of a son
coming from a father, full of grace and truth. Do you seek truth?
Do you want grace? Look here. The Word, the Son, brings life.
The Word, the Son, empowers us to be children of God, and

to find our way in life, to come to the fulfillment of all we are meant to be.

The Word became flesh and lived among us. Why? Why not just another prophet? Why not another sign in the heavens? Why not a more direct and clear text?

We might ask instead: What could convey God's self-expression better, more clearly? What greater self-revelation could there be? What more could God do to express his love than to share our life, our joys and sorrows, our hopes and limitations, to show us what human life can be? What greater text could be given than the one written in flesh and blood? What greater love could be shown than to lay down one's life, to become vulnerable, dependent on us, as dependent as a newborn baby on its mother?

The Word became flesh and lived among us. The divine lot is thrown in with ours, in order to show us the way to the divine, in order to reveal God's love. That enduring love is what we forever bow before. And sing about.

> From his fullness we have all received, grace upon grace. The law indeed was given through Moses; grace and truth came through Jesus Christ. No one has ever seen God. It is God the only Son, who is close to the Father's heart, who has made him known.
> (John 1:16–18)

Four
The Holy Ordinary

And the child's father and mother were amazed at what was being said about him. Then Simeon blessed them and said to his mother Mary, "This child is destined for the falling and the rising of many in Israel, and to be a sign that will be opposed so that the inner thoughts of many will be revealed—and a sword will pierce your own soul too." (Luke 2:33–35)

• • • • • • •

What comes to your mind when you hear the word *family?* The word carries so many feelings and concepts, warmth and pain. Personal experience, social reality, statistics, and politics collide in our minds and decisions. There is so much complexity and diversity in that one word.

We can speak of a diversity of form. There are all kinds of families. We think of our biological family, of course. But then there are the intentional families we gather around ourselves. We think of parents and children, or one-parent families, a single mom or dad struggling to create a home. We think of spouses without children, or domestic partnerships, roommates, households of all kinds. All centers of meaning, concern, friendship, community.

We can also speak of a diversity of experience. On one hand, we can imagine the most ideal experiences. Families that always nourish each other, support each other, giving children the best possible start in life. On the other hand, we can just as easily imagine experiences of abuse and violence, and we can imagine the pain and the need for healing in those experiences. We can imagine those experiences and everything in between: hopes, successes, failures, and struggles.

For better or worse, we begin with family. We're formed within significant relationships that accompany us, care for us, and annoy us. We learn from those relationships, and sometimes we have to unlearn what we've been taught. We need to let go, forgive, understand, and accept. We also need to search out, form, and create family for ourselves and others.

In all of this diversity, all this struggle, what can Jesus' family offer us? What does this "holy family" show us?

Now after they had left, an angel of the Lord appeared to Joseph in a dream and said, "Get up, take the child and his mother, and flee to Egypt, and remain there until I tell you; for Herod is about to search for the child, to destroy him." Then Joseph got up, took the child and his mother by night, and went to Egypt, and remained there until the death of Herod. This was to fulfill what had been spoken by the Lord through the prophet, "Out of Egypt I have called my son."

When Herod died, an angel of the Lord suddenly appeared in a dream to Joseph in Egypt and said, " Get up, take the child and his mother, and go to the land of Israel, for those who were seeking the child's life are dead." Then Joseph got up, took the child and his mother, and went to the land of Israel. But when he heard that Archelaus was ruling over Judea in place of his father Herod, he was afraid to go there. And after being warned in a dream, he went away to the district of Galilee. There he made his home in a town called Nazareth, so that what had been spoken through the prophets might be fulfilled, "He will be called a Nazorean." (Matthew 2:13-15, 19-23)

The Scriptures don't share much about Jesus' family life, but we do catch glimpses. We see Joseph's leadership and protection as he brings his family down to Egypt and back again in the midst of crisis, alert to their needs. We see Mary's strength and courage in her ability to take on the unknown and the risks of her life with underlying trust, bearing it all, bearing that sword, being that anchor for her family.

Then, perhaps, we see a little adolescent rebelliousness when a twelve-year-old Jesus decides to stay in Jerusalem without letting Mom or Dad know. We see parental concern even later in life: Mary, pushing Jesus along toward his ministry at the wedding in Cana, then trying to pull him back from ministry when he started to become controversial, sending other relatives to get him and bring him home. One day she's letting go, realizing he has to live his own life, his own calling; another day she's afraid for him, trying to protect him, trying to hang on.

It all seems so normal, so ordinary. That's one thing we learn from this holy family: the holiness of what is ordinary. This family points us, not to something ideal or unreal, but to the ordinary. Even when we have extraordinary challenges to face, God comes to us in ordinary ways. We don't need to look beyond where we are. We don't need to have someone else's family. We need to go to what we have and see it as it is. We need to appreciate and understand it, learn from it, grow through it. As we do, and as we separate out the good from the bad, we'll discover more of who we are. We will discover our own capacity to build family for others.

When they had finished everything required by the law
of the Lord, they returned to Galilee, to their own town
of Nazareth. The child grew and became strong, filled
with wisdom; and the favor of God was upon him. (Luke
2:39-40)

From Jesus' own words and example, we might imagine what
he brought with him from his family into his ministry. When he
weeps at his friend Lazarus's tomb, when he shows compassion
to the outsider or those in need, when he shows us his heart —
can we imagine what he saw in Mary's example, what he saw
in her heart? When we hear his storytelling, when we hear the
parable of the prodigal son, when we see his concern for justice,
his prophetic zeal, his strength — can we imagine the lessons
he learned from Joseph?

Then his mother and his brothers came; and standing
outside, they sent to him and called him. A crowd was
sitting around him; and they said to him, "Your mother
and your brothers and sisters are outside, asking for
you." And he replied, "Who are my mother and my
brothers?" And looking at those who sat around him, he
said, "Here are my mother and my brothers! Whoever
does the will of God is my brother and sister and
mother." (Mark 3:31-35)

Yet another thing we learn from the holy family: we are
members of it.

When Mary, frightened for Jesus, came with relatives to take
him away from the crowds and bring him back home, he had to
say it: No — there is no going back into safety. I know who I

am; I know what I'm called to do. I know the purpose God has given me in life. But his way of saying that was to look at those around him, listening to his words, hungering for his message. He points to his disciples, those he's bringing into his inner circle, and says: This is my family. Everyone who listens to me, who seeks to do God's will in their lives, *"is my brother and sister and mother."* That includes us.

We have a spiritual family: all those brothers and sisters of ours, who from the beginning have followed the Lord's path through history, and those who are on it now. We can go to one another for support and encouragement. We can go to Mary and Joseph for inspiration and example. We can go to our brother Jesus for healing and strength, and for the knowledge of who we are as God's children.

In Celtic spirituality, one hears of the *anam cara*, the "soul friend," the one with whom we can be our true selves. With a soul friend, we can share the whole journey, good and bad. We can share profound truths and insights, as well as the inconsequential, ordinary events of our life. Both are important for intimacy, because it's in the inconsequential and ordinary stuff of life that we grow. That's where we find the most meaningful, the most extraordinary lessons. That's where we find family.

Jesus, Mary, and Joseph are pointing us there, and they meet us there — in the ordinary. And God can use it all, heal it all, bless it all, as we bring it all to him.

The Feast

Five
Perfectly Human

· · · · · · ·

There's a saying from the Twelve Step movement: "I'm not perfect, but I am perfectly human."

Holiness is about being real. It's about becoming more real. Holiness is not being immune from problems. It's how we deal with our problems, respond to them, and transform them. Holiness is found in how we use our gifts in the face of all life brings us.

One of the Gospel passages we've looked at already is the prologue to John's Gospel, with that verse that's so familiar to us: *"The Word became flesh and lived among us"* (1:14). Sometimes we hear how that verse might more literally be translated as the Word "pitched its tent among us." That helps to make the point that the Incarnation, the mystery of God coming to dwell with us, was not a one-time event. God made a commitment to the good and the bad, to the highs and lows, to all the commonplace reality of human life. That's where the Incarnation gets played out. That's what God raises up to himself and makes holy.

> Now every year his parents went to Jerusalem for the festival of the Passover. And when he was twelve years old, they went up as usual for the festival. When the festival was ended and they started to return, the boy Jesus stayed behind in Jerusalem, but his parents did not know it. Assuming that he was in the group of travelers, they went a day's journey. Then they started to look for him among their relatives and friends. When they did not find him, they returned to Jerusalem to search

for him. After three days they found him in the temple,
sitting among the teachers, listening to them and asking
them questions. And all who heard him were amazed
at his understanding and his answers. When his parents
saw him they were astonished; and his mother said to
him, "Child, why have you treated us like this? Look,
your father and I have been searching for you in great
anxiety." He said to them, "Why were you searching
for me? Did you not know that I must be in my Father's
house?" But they did not understand what he said
to them. Then he went down with them and came
to Nazareth, and was obedient to them. His mother
treasured all these things in her heart.

And Jesus increased in wisdom and in years, and in
divine and human favor. (Luke 2:41–52)

Young Jesus in the temple. God even raised up adolescence
to himself, and everything that goes along with it. We think
of all those questions and struggles, those hormones and emotions. And we think of Jesus having to navigate those same tur-
bulent waters. We think of all the relationships and connections
that guide our growth: immediate family, extended family, faith
community, friends. We think of the ways they give us support
and the ways they fail us, or we fail them. We bring each other
consolation and distress, relief and heartache. How easy it is to
see that we aren't perfect, but we are perfectly human.

I once heard someone speak about her marriage. She said that,
like life, her relationship has had many peaks and valleys. But,
she said, there was a bridge over the valleys, bringing her from
peak to peak. And the name of the bridge is commitment. That
image may not account for all the complexities that people face,

but it points to a deeper level of promise and steadfastness that underlies our growth. If a life is to thrive, it must come to know a level of commitment and dedication that sustains us through success and failure.

God pitched a tent. God made a commitment. And so God is found in our imperfect humanity. God will work in our imperfect relationships and families. God will be there in our wounded neighborhoods and workplaces and communities of faith, inviting us to greater health and wholeness. God is ready to meet us in all those places.

> See what love the Father has given us, that we should be called children of God; and that is what we are. The reason the world does not know us is that it did not know him. Beloved, we are God's children now; what we will be has not yet been revealed. What we do know is this: when he is revealed, we will be like him, for we will see him as he is. . . . Beloved, if our hearts do not condemn us, we have boldness before God; and we receive from him whatever we ask, because we obey his commandments and do what pleases him.
>
> And this is his commandment, that we should believe in the name of his Son Jesus Christ and love one another, just as he has commanded us. All who obey his commandments abide in him, and he abides in them. And by this we know that he abides in us, by the Spirit that he has given us. (1 John 3:1–2, 21–24)

Years ago, when I was studying social work, I ran across something called "family systems theory." It says a family is like any organic system, from the single cell to a massive forest, or even like inorganic systems, from molecules to galaxies. All systems share certain characteristics that can be applied to any human system, like a family.

Interconnectedness is an example. When one part or member of a system changes, the whole system changes and adapts. When one person changes, becomes motivated, or grows, it affects the whole.

The Feast

When there's a problem, isn't our tendency to blame? We blame everyone else. *They* need to change. Well, maybe they do need to change, but *we* can't change others. We can only change ourselves. And that will have an effect on everything else, because we're all interconnected.

When we take care of ourselves first, when we care for our personal and spiritual growth, we become agents of change. That personal growth will subtly have its effects on our families and communities. That's true of systems within systems, too. When two parents take care of themselves, take care of their relationship, it will affect the whole family.

Another characteristic of systems is found in the law of *entropy*: unless energy is put into a system, the system will start to disintegrate. The energy will dissipate.

Who is putting energy into our relationships, families, communities? Are we energizers? How do we use our gifts? Are we claiming our power to bring joy and happiness to others? In the face of the uncertainties of life, do we go numb? Are we absent? Or do we go forward in faith? Faith is energy. It builds up the system. When we are responsive and concerned about others who are in need, we're building up the system. When we go out of our way to help, or when we offer our wisdom and encouragement, or when we are cheerful givers, we're building up the system. When we do our part to help manage the family, or facilitate communication, or plan celebrations, or cultivate friendship, or serve the community in any way, we're creating more energy for a living organism. We're building up God's people.

We don't have to wait for anyone else to act. We have our own source of energy. Here, though, is the difference between us and just any physical system: we have a never-ending energy source to go to, a never-ending supply, a higher power — the Spirit. That's what St. John tells us in his first epistle: it is the Spirit who makes us children of God. That's our core identity. Our human families, or communities, or institutions can't give us that. The Spirit does.

We rely on the Spirit to guide us wherever we are on this human journey. It's there that the Word made flesh finds us, teaches us, and leads us. We aren't perfect, but we are perfectly human. And that's all we need to be.

Six
Ponder

When the angels had left them and gone into heaven,
the shepherds said to one another, "Let us go now
to Bethlehem and see this thing that has taken place,
which the Lord has made known to us." So they went
with haste and found Mary and Joseph, and the child
lying in the manger. When they saw this, they made
known what had been told them about this child; and
all who heard it were amazed at what the shepherds
told them. But Mary treasured all these words and

pondered them in her heart. The shepherds returned, glorifying and praising God for all they had heard and seen, as it had been told them. (Luke 2:15–21)

• • • • • • •

I heard the spiritual writer Ronald Rolheiser speak about these verses once. He dwelt on these words: *"But Mary treasured all these words and pondered them in her heart."* Other translations use the words *kept* and *reflected.* Sometimes we think of *reflecting* as identical to *thinking.* It's a head thing, an intellectual exercise. We may think of a good memory and replay it again and again in our head; or we may wallow in a bad memory. In either case, we can get stuck in the past. We try to recapture a good feeling, or we stew in remorse.

The point Rolheiser made was that this "pondering" or "reflecting" that the Gospel speaks of is not just thinking about something. It's not just a head thing. Interestingly, the word translated here as *pondered* is not a common word in the Scriptures. In fact, it is only used of Mary in this instance. According to Rolheiser, the best way to understand this kind of reflecting is in the sense of "holding" or "carrying" something. One holds something in tension, and one "carries" that tension in a way that transforms it.

We also can see that meaning reflected in the Latin roots of the word *flectare,* which is to "bend," to "turn." *Re-flectare* is to bend and turn again and again. One might think of a jeweler who turns a fine gem over and over to appreciate its many facets. Or think of a plant that is growing toward the light, bending again and again toward that source of light, so that it can flourish.

Reflecting, in this sense, is a search for awareness. It is becoming more aware of the deeper meanings in our experience. It is learning and growing through our experience, listening for God's voice, allowing God's light into our experience to guide us.

To reflect on whatever life throws at us, good or bad, will mean to hold and question it with a trust and faith that allows us to *pass through* it. Not to avoid or to be defeated by it, but to pass through it to another level of understanding and peace. We transcend it. We reach another plateau and are stronger because of it.

Mary is pondering at the Annunciation, when she questions the angel, *"How can this be?"* (Luke 1:34). Then, at the foot of the cross in silence, we see her pondering again.

We can think of times in life when we seem to have no choice but to ponder. A young couple I know thought they would never have a child of their own, and then found themselves suddenly preparing for a new baby. Another friend found himself, after a downturn in his job sector, struggling to begin again in a new profession. I visited the parents of a college student I know who kept vigil for many weeks in a hospital ICU waiting room after their son was in a car accident. He, with much therapy, recovered. They came to know another couple in that same waiting room and accompanied them as they learned that their child, who was also in an accident, had such severe brain damage that there would be no recovery.

How will these experiences affect their lives, their choices, their future? Will they get stuck? Will they *re-flect?* Will they "pass through"? Will they, with the help of faith and trust, bend toward the light?

Reflection as a spiritual exercise is not meant to be something that we call upon in extremis. It is meant to be a pillar of life. We will be able to call upon the fruit of reflection in times of greatest need because we have developed a pattern of pondering, a habit of bending toward the light.

An example of such a spiritual discipline is the Ignatian "Daily Examen of Consciousness." This refers to a basic review of one's day in the light of faith. What went wrong? Where did I fail to live up to my calling and need to ask for mercy? What went right? How did I experience the fullness of life and so need to express thanks for God's blessings? Reflection deepens our awareness of the good in our lives. Again, a gratitude journal comes to mind, as a way of fostering a healthier outlook. Simply writing down things that we are grateful for, that happened that day, opens our eyes to the many small blessings that color our lives.

> The LORD spoke to Moses, saying: Speak to Aaron and his sons, saying, Thus you shall bless the Israelites: You shall say to them,
> > The LORD bless you and keep you;
> > the LORD make his face to shine upon you, and be gracious to you;
> > the LORD lift up his countenance upon you, and give you peace.
> So they shall put my name on the Israelites, and I will bless them. (Numbers 6:22–27)

The blessing of Aaron in the book of Numbers isn't just any blessing. It sums up Israel's understanding of God's relationship to them, the meaning of the covenant. *"The Lord make his face to shine upon you, and be gracious to you!"* How many times, in the darkest times, have we felt like the Lord's face was hidden from us? We saw no meaning or purpose, no light.

But the Lord is not hiding. God sent a Savior so that we'd know that no matter what his light will shine, his light will bring meaning. The Lord will *"lift up his countenance upon you, and give you peace."* This peace, of course, is the biblical *shalom*. The word in

Hebrew conveys a sense of completeness, wholeness, and harmony. The kindness of the Lord brings everything we need.

No matter what time or place we are in, what darkness we must face, what tension we must hold, we can take our lead from Mary. We can ponder — reflecting, with faith and trust in the Lord, who will accompany us, transform us, and bring us through it all, to that lasting peace.

Seven
A Slave or a Child

> Long ago God spoke to our ancestors in many and various ways by the prophets, but in these last days he has spoken to us by a Son, whom he appointed heir of all things, through whom he also created the worlds. He is the reflection of God's glory and the exact imprint of God's very being, and he sustains all things by his powerful word. When he had made purification for sins, he sat down at the right hand of the Majesty on high. (Hebrews 1:1–3)

* * * * * * *

I remember a movie on television I saw when I was young. I wish I could remember the title, but it really doesn't matter. There have been many films over the years like it. This is how I remember it: the world is coming to an end. The earth is losing its orbit and slowly moving closer to the sun. There is nothing anyone can do about it. As humanity awaits the inevitable, social structures start to break down. Nothing matters, and so there are those who loot, riot, and rape. They devolve into a hedonist waste. And yet, there are others who remain heroic to the end. They want their last days to be the most honorable in their lives. Because nothing matters, they find a new perspective on life. They give for the sake of giving; they seek beauty for the sake of beauty.

What makes for such a different response? How would we respond? We don't have to wait for the apocalypse to find out. We have our own little dramas and cataclysms to deal with. What do they draw out of us?

Every day we respond to the world around us. Some are stuck in anger and denial. They've lost a sense of meaning. They walk over people in order to get what they want. Others open themselves to discover the meaning. They seek to contribute to the beauty around them. They want to serve someone; they want to serve the good.

Some get their sense of worth from the things they own. They are controlled by their need to have more. They judge others by what they have or by what they can get from them. Others choose not to be controlled by materialism. They enjoy things for the good they can offer; they use things to enhance their lives and relationships. They are generous with all they have.

Often we are wronged, hurt by another. We are forced to deal with the injustice of the world around us. Some allow bitterness to grow and let it eat away at them. They are controlled by their resentment, stuck in their pain. Others choose to work through their pain. They don't allow others' choices to control them. They decide to enter a process of forgiveness and acceptance.

Where do we see ourselves in this dichotomy? Most likely the answer is not simple. We may see an interplay of light and

The Feast

shadow. But we must ask: What is influencing our heart? What path are we choosing to travel?

> But when the fullness of time had come, God sent his Son, born of a woman, born under the law, in order to redeem those who were under the law, so that we might receive adoption as children. And because you are children, God has sent the Spirit of his Son into our hearts, crying, "Abba! Father!" So you are no longer a slave but a child, and if a child then also an heir, through God. (Galatians 4:4–7)

St. Paul, in his letter to the Galatians, uses a stark image: the difference between being a slave or a child, a slave or an heir. The Galatians had heard and accepted the Good News that Paul preached to them, but they were still immature in their faith. They had quickly regressed to their earlier system of beliefs, their earlier way of relating to God and their world. Paul confronts them with a stark choice: who will be in charge of your life? The implications are great. Will it be the stars, the fates? Will it be the religious laws and rules that others are trying to impose on you? Will you go back to your fears? Will they immobilize you?

Paul tells them that if they go back to what they were before they knew Christ, they will be no better than a slave. Christ came into the world to free us. When we join our lives to him, we have the free gift of the Spirit. We are children of the one true God. We have been given the power to call God "Abba" as Jesus did. We are called into the same relationship of intimacy with God as Jesus had. It is this intimacy that transforms us into a free people, free to live life fully.

You do not have to live in fear of any other being or force. You do not fear God as if he were an alien taskmaster. You are not under the power of others. You are not under the power of sin, or death, or anything else that can oppress human beings. Now you can see the things that really matter in life. You are a son. You are a daughter.

Paul is convinced that when you are not "under the law," but under the love of God through Christ, it will make all the difference. You are a child. You are an heir. You know you are loved no matter what. And you will love. You will find happiness. Even as you make your way through a life that knows grief and death, you will know you are a child.

The Feast

> How beautiful upon the mountains
>   are the feet of the messenger who announces peace,
> who brings good news,
>   who announces salvation,
>   who says to Zion, "Your God reigns."
> Listen! Your sentinels lift up their voices,
>   together they sing for joy;
> for in plain sight they see
>   the return of the Lord to Zion.
> Break forth together into singing,
>   you ruins of Jerusalem;
> for the Lord has comforted his people,
>   he has redeemed Jerusalem.
> The Lord has bared his holy arm
>   before the eyes of all the nations;
> and all the ends of the earth shall see
>   the salvation of our God. (Isaiah 52:7-10)

We may not be able to say we're fully there yet. We may not be that mature. We may not be able to claim we've fully absorbed the Good News and its implications. In all the dramas and cataclysms of life, we may not always be able to say, I'm the one who serves freely, gives generously, searches faithfully. I'm the one who forgives fully, loves purely, dies gracefully. More likely, we will be able to identify with those Galatians, who hear and yet are quick to forget. We know what it is like to regress at times into the slavery of bitterness, materialism, resentment, fear.

What do we do to become a child, an heir? It is, rather, what God does. God has chosen to make us heirs. What we do is accept and nurture that Good News. We receive God's Word and let it germinate in our lives. We nurture, not the slave, but that child. We listen within to the voice of the Spirit crying, "Abba." And the slave slowly loses its hold, and the daughter, the son we are, the person we were created to be, stands up in power and grace.

The Season
Epiphanies

I salute you! There is nothing I can give you which you
have not; but there is much that, while I cannot give,
you can take.

No heaven can come to us unless our hearts find rest in
it today. Take Heaven!

No peace lies in the future which is not hidden in the
present moment. Take Peace!

The gloom of the world is but a shadow; behind it, yet
within our reach is joy. There is radiance and glory in
the darkness, could we but see; and to see, we have
only to look. I beseech you to look!

Life is so generous a giver, but we, judging its gifts by
their covering, cast them away as ugly or heavy or
hard. Remove the covering, and you will find beneath
it a living splendor, woven of love, by wisdom, with
power. Welcome it, grasp it, and you touch the Angel's
hand that brings it to you.

Life is so full of meaning and of purpose, so full of
beauty—beneath its covering—that you will find that
earth but cloaks your heaven. Courage, then to claim it:
that is all!

And so, at this Christmas time, I greet you, with the
prayer that for you, now and forever, the day breaks
and the shadows flee away.

—FRA GIOVANNI GIOCONDO

One
Breaking Barriers

The abundance of the sea shall be brought to you,
 the wealth of the nations shall come to you.
A multitude of camels shall cover you,
 the young camels of Midian and Ephah;
 all those from Sheba shall come.
They shall bring gold and frankincense,
 and shall proclaim the praise of the LORD.
(Isaiah 60:5-6)

● ● ● ● ● ● ●

The prophets of Israel were not only interested in what God was doing for the chosen people, but also in what God would do for the world through them. If they didn't get in God's way, God would use them, and the other nations would come to see divine truth and light in the midst of darkness. They would be drawn to that light. They would travel far to find those spiritual riches and would bring their own riches as gifts. It would be a time of divine insight and clarity—an epiphany.

The word *epiphany* may not be a part of our everyday vocabulary, but hopefully we can all relate to its meaning. The beauty of the word reflects the beauty of the experience. The Merriam-Webster dictionary gives a simple definition: "a moment in which you suddenly see or understand something in a new or very clear way... an illuminating discovery, realization, or disclosure."

If you have a difficult time trying to think of examples of such moments, you could always think of your favorite movies. Films, like many art forms, often present a distilled portrayal of human experience. Moments of epiphany are highlighted. Moments of clarity, revelation, and decision are turning points in the story; they point the way to something deeper, something that makes the character's life a true adventure. A problem is engaged, an insight is grasped, a test is met.

At one time I studied film at a major film school in Los Angeles. I remember seeing a movie with one of my film school friends that depicted a main character's religious conversion. The scene tried to convey mystical and supernatural elements, but seemed rather conventional to me, hokey even. Later, after critiquing the movie on a number of levels, my friend wanted to talk more about that scene. He wasn't religious at all, but he was a searcher. He wanted to talk about the kinds of experiences the film was trying to explore. He wanted to know if people really have those kinds of experiences. The discussion got more personal. We talked about spirituality and how God impacts people's lives. At one point he said: "I wish I could have that kind of experience." He was basically opening himself up to the possibility of understanding the place of belief in people's lives. He wanted to be touched by transcendence in some way. He wanted to find something that could give him that kind of meaning. An epiphany.

We had moved from talking about a movie to talking about our lives. We moved from the superficial to the real. When we are able to drop our defenses and be more honest with ourselves, when we open ourselves to what is beyond ourselves, to God and the spiritual insights that God wants to give us, we are on fertile ground for an epiphany.

In former generations this mystery was not made known to humankind, as it has now been revealed to his holy

apostles and prophets by the Spirit: that is, the Gentiles
have become fellow heirs, members of the same body,
and sharers in the promise in Christ Jesus through the
gospel. (Ephesians 3:5-6)

St. Paul saw the insights of prophets like Isaiah taking place in
the Christian communities that he formed. He saw it happening
in a literal and drastic way. Gentiles were coming to faith in
Christ and were being incorporated into one community with
Jewish believers. God was breaking down religious, social, and
racial barriers that existed between people and making them
one in Christ.

Not everyone in the church was happy about these
developments, though. To them, the unclean was being grafted
onto what was pure. How could that be God's plan? The New
Testament's insights were not built on ivory-tower reflections.
They were being played out in the common experiences of
ordinary people in their communities: Jews and Gentiles were
coming around the same table to celebrate the memory of Jesus.
An unthinkable, impossible thing was happening.

The barriers that kept people apart, fearful, at war — these
were falling away as people became united in Christ, members
of one body. People were finding what they were looking for
in God's revelation to Israel. This was something foretold by
prophets, and now it was happening. Paul reflected on that and
said: Look at what God is doing. Let's not get in God's way with
our illusions and fears. Let's cooperate with him. We are the
epiphany now.

Of course, we do get in God's way all the time. God tears
down the walls and we start repairing them. We return to the
safety of our prejudices and our illusions. Dorothy Day told

the story of one of her early confidants. He grew up as a little Jewish boy in a Christian neighborhood in New York City in the 1920s. Once, on his way home from school, he was jumped by a gang of older boys who beat and kicked him. He heard one of them say, "They killed Jesus." When he got home, his mother cleaned him up. As she held and rocked him to sleep, the boy raised his lips to her ear and asked: "Who's Jesus?"

Sometimes the darkness in the world is obvious and cruel; sometimes it is subtle and sophisticated, even respectable. Yet something in human beings keeps searching for divine truth and light in the midst of darkness. It seeks fertile ground for insight and discovery. It wants to get out of God's way and cooperate with his work. It wants a spiritual breakthrough. It wants an epiphany.

That happens because God's light breaks through to us, because God's light is at work in us. As God used the chosen people, as God used the early church, God will use us to bring his light to others. And people will be drawn to that light.

Two
Extra Ordinary

In the time of King Herod, after Jesus was born in Bethlehem of Judea, wise men from the East came to Jerusalem, asking, "Where is the child who has been born king of the Jews? For we observed his star at its rising, and have come to pay him homage." When King Herod heard this, he was frightened, and all Jerusalem with him; and calling together all the chief priests and scribes of the people, he inquired of them where the Messiah was to be born. They told him, "In Bethlehem of Judea; for so it has been written by the prophet:

'And you, Bethlehem, in the land of Judah,
   are by no means least among the rulers of Judah;
for from you shall come a ruler
   who is to shepherd my people Israel.'"
(Matthew 2:1-6)

· · · · · · · ·

In Christian theology, an epiphany refers to a manifestation of Christ. God takes the initiative here. God is revealing something, Christ is mysteriously being manifested. Something beyond us is breaking through to us, and there are those who get it! People, however faintly, are willing to see it, ready to listen.

A classic example of this from the Christmas story is the visit of the Magi, learned seekers from the East who appear in Bethlehem. Some churches celebrate the Feast of Epiphany. It's traditionally observed on January 6, the "Twelfth Day" after Christmas, but on some liturgical calendars it's transferred to one of the Sundays during the Christmas season. The feast commemorates the coming of the Magi. For some cultures this is the day for gift giving and unique celebrations. In certain Eastern churches, there is a tradition on this feast of throwing a cross into a lake while parishioners compete by diving into the water to find it. Someone suddenly emerges from the depths, gasping for breath, holding high the cross — a stunning image and symbol of epiphany.

Two things about the story of the Magi can relate to our personal epiphanies. First, there is a star. God sends a star

that's more than a star. It's a sign. It has a message. The Magi
are different because they look up and see the stars. They are
searching and sensitive to creation.

We are surrounded by stars, but do we see the signs? Do we
hear the message? There is a way to live life where one never
looks up at the stars. The Magi are called "wise" because they
look up! They realize that there is more to life. They believe
there is a reality beyond us that wants to communicate to us.
They want to stop, to listen, to be receptive.

Where is the star the Lord may be sending us? Is it in a flash
of insight that may help us solve a problem, or that inspires us
to make life better? Is it someone who has been an example to
us through their love or goodness, or someone who is able to
slow us down so that we can appreciate life? Is it an experience
of God's creation that brings us to a place of wonder and awe?
Is it a challenge that pushes us to grow or change? A dream that
fires our imagination?

It may come in many forms, but somewhere in our lives, we
are being invited to go beyond ourselves and what we know. Or
we are being invited to go deeper, to see and appreciate where
we are now in a new way. We need to "look up"—to be attentive
to the signs.

Second, the Magi not only saw the star—they *followed* it. That
doesn't go without saying. There are plenty of times throughout
history, and most likely in our own lives, where the star shone,
the light appeared, the idea flashed, the insight came, the
message was given, and nothing happened. Nothing happened
because no one followed.

It's hard to follow the star, to get up and move. It's hard to
step out of old habits and build new ones. That's because there
are Herods out there. There are obstacles and threats. You'll

have any number of reasons to stay in your comfort zone. The Magi prepared for their journey; they made plans and gathered resources. They followed through despite the risks. That makes them wise, too.

And where does it lead them? How surprised were these seekers when the star — their hope, their quest for something better, for meaning, for salvation — did not lead them to Herod's palace or to other high places befitting their stature, but to the backwater of Bethlehem? What did they think when they were led to a stable? God's plans for us may lead through the spectacular, or may just as easily lead through the most humble and ordinary circumstances.

This phase of the Christmas season tells us: Look up! The stars are being sent not just at Christmastime but throughout the year. Recognize those flashes and insights, those invitations to more life. And follow where they lead. Don't let them pass by. Follow them to the depths of murky waters if necessary. There will be epiphanies: extraordinary or ordinary. There are places where Christ is being manifested. We will be guided to see his presence in our lives, so that we become more like that human person he is calling us to be. We will emerge from the murkiness, filling our lungs with air, into the sunlight.

Three
Three Gifts

Lift up your eyes and look around;
   they all gather together, they come to you;
your sons shall come from far away,
   and your daughters shall be carried on their nurses'
arms.
Then you shall see and be radiant;
   your heart shall thrill and rejoice. (Isaiah 60:4-5)

* * * * * * *

Every year we hear the same stories. Mary, Joseph, shepherds, angels, foreigners — all on different journeys and all converging in Bethlehem. The stories, carols, church services, school plays: the same every year but also different. Different because we are different every year. Every year we bring ourselves to these stories, and we're always changing. We've had different experiences, we're asking different questions. We'll see something new, hear a detail we never noticed. A word, a phrase, a meaning will come to our aid in a new way.

The power in these stories is that they have the capacity to meet us wherever we are in life. They keep addressing human questions and doubts. They keep speaking to the world's tensions and crises. The journeys keep crossing paths at Bethlehem.

An epiphany is defined as a manifestation of Christ. Franciscan author Richard Rohr, in *Everything Belongs*, gives his own twist to that definition: an epiphany is a place where God is both hidden and revealed.[6] Perfectly hidden and perfectly revealed — like the manger or the cross. Not everyone is looking for those epiphanies, not everyone sees. But those who do will *"gather together."* Their journeys converge in Bethlehem. Their hearts *"thrill and rejoice."*

> Then Herod secretly called for the wise men and learned from them the exact time when the star had appeared. Then he sent them to Bethlehem, saying, "Go and search diligently for the child; and when you have found him, bring me word so that I may also go and pay him homage." When they had heard the king, they set out; and there, ahead of them, went the star that they had seen at its rising, until it stopped over the place where the child was. When they saw that the star had stopped, they were overwhelmed with joy. On entering the house, they saw the child with Mary his mother; and they knelt down and paid him homage. Then, opening their treasure chests, they offered him gifts of gold, frankincense, and myrrh. (Matthew 2:7-11)

In Luke's Gospel, it is the Jewish poor, the shepherds, who first see and recognize this birth as a manifestation of God in their midst. Perhaps this reflects the experience of Luke's community and its emphasis on Jesus' outreach to the marginal ones. In Matthew's Gospel, it's the Magi, these Gentile outsiders, who see a mysterious star and follow it. They recognize that the promises made to the chosen people are being fulfilled. How unlikely that they would be the ones to see and understand, while others who are much closer to the revelation are indifferent, or even hostile, to it. Herod, as we've seen, is confronted by the same mysterious clues, but instead of searching for the star himself, he's threatened by it. All he sees is his own power. All he cares about preserving is his own worldly authority. That's all that matters. No epiphany for him.

It's the Magi who seek out a different kind of king. The symbolism of their first gift is apparent. Gold is a gift for royalty. They had just left Herod's palace with all its trappings of power, yet here is where they leave their gold — in a stable. They recognize something. They say: here is where the real power is. Here is what really matters. That takes a certain kind of seeing, a certain kind of vision.

Things have not changed much as far as power goes. We still hear stories of regimes — governments, bureaucracies, managers, supervisors — who care only about preserving themselves, even at the expense of their own people. Instead of seeing their position as a way of serving the good of others, they act as if they don't care how others suffer. The point is keeping their power.

Whether we run a government or a household, a company or a personal calendar, we have our own gold, our own influence, our own gifts to give. We have a place to exercise our power. Where do we bring our gold? Will we bring it to the Lord, the source of that gift? When we recognize Christ's sovereignty in our lives, when his way has priority in our lives, we're following that star. Epiphanies can happen.

Frankincense is the priestly gift. It's the gift of prayer, worship, devotion. It recognizes Christ as the source of priestly power in our lives. It's easier to see where we have worldly power or can exercise external authority over others. We may not appreciate the spiritual power we have as well. How do we burn the gift of frankincense in our lives?

Who receives our reverence, honor, prayer, study? Some people are much more interested in burning incense before their stock portfolios than before the manger. What we reverence will gain our allegiance. What we contemplate will determine our goals.

We need to recognize what is worthy of our attention, our concern, our time. With prayer comes recognition. With prayer comes the ability to discern darkness and light, delusion and self-honesty. With prayer comes awareness of our need for repentance and renewal. With prayer comes conviction to act in justice and compassion. This priestly prayer aligns ourselves with the source of our well-being and will radiate well-being to others.

And then there is the precious ointment myrrh. One of its uses at the time was the anointing of a body for burial. This is the gift of one's whole self. It is the prophetic gift of sacrifice, suffering, and hardship in service to the love of God and neighbor. It is the ointment of love. Who will we anoint with that gift of love? Will it flow freely, or will we hoard it until it has lost its fragrance and energy?

In sacramental churches, after baptism a believer is anointed with perfumed oil, "as priest, prophet, and king." Then, at confirmation, one is anointed as a sign of a new outpouring of the Spirit. One is anointed, too, at times of illness and physical or emotional diminishment. It's a way of saying that everything in that person's life—relationships, work, vocation, even their hardship—is "anointed" to manifest Christ's love. In some places, when a new church building is dedicated, the walls are anointed. Everything that community does—its teaching, service, outreach—is called to express the prophetic gift. The oil must flow everywhere. Everything must speak of the gift of love: God's love poured out to us in Jesus and our love flowing out to the world.

As Jesus is the epiphany of God in our world, so we become the possibility for epiphany to others. As the manger manifests the way God works in the world, so our lives can manifest Christ's power working in us. It begins, as it did with the Magi, when we allow the light of his star, the light of his love, to inspire and guide us. Our stories will converge on Bethlehem. Our hearts will *"thrill and rejoice."* We will come to see that the gifts we bring are the gifts that we have been given, to be used for his glory.

Four

Hope Anytime

• • • • • • •

In *Image and Likeness: Religious Visions in American Film Classics,* the film scholar John R. May tells of how a particular line of dialogue from a film held an inordinate claim on his memory. It came, not from a great classic, but from what some would consider a rather forgettable movie from the 1970s: *Beneath the Planet of the Apes.* "When may we hope to be free?" asks the imprisoned Cornelius, the ape protagonist. His simian captor responds: "You may hope any time you wish."[7]

Even in a B-movie you can find a great line like that. Since reading May's reflection, I've never forgotten it either. Even in the worst of circumstances, hope is born. In fact, the worse the times, the brighter the hope seems. Negativity and cynicism try to do their worst to us at times, and the effects of such dispar-agement are easily found. Yet these places where things look as bad as they can get — these are also the places we find the greatest examples of hope. It's the hope that begins something new. It sets us on a new path toward change and a more just world.

From the beginning of Advent, we've reflected on how hope is not mere optimism or wishful thinking. It is not a passive form of waiting. It is an active vision that captures and energizes us. It empowers us because it is grounded in something real — a relationship of trust. And we can hope anytime we want.

> See, I am sending my messenger to prepare the way before me, and the Lord whom you seek will suddenly come to his temple. The messenger of the covenant in whom you delight—indeed, he is coming, says the LORD of hosts. But who can endure the day of his coming, and who can stand when he appears? For he is like a refiner's fire and like fullers' soap; he will sit as a refiner and purifier of silver, and he will purify the descendants of Levi and refine them like gold and silver, until they present offerings to the LORD in righteousness. (Malachi 3:1-3)

The prophet Malachi appeared at a time of discouragement for the chosen people. They had survived the exile under the Babylonians and were back in their homeland. In what should have been a time of gratitude and renewed fidelity to God's law, Malachi saw the old patterns beginning again, the attitudes that had gotten the people in trouble in the past. The same old injustices, abuses, and indifference were creeping back into the culture. The prophet confronts his people, but is met with the cynical retort: *"Where is the God of justice?"* (Malachi 2:17).

Malachi's response is that the Lord's way is being prepared. He will come to his temple as a refining fire. In the midst of your ingratitude and failure and discouragement, God will be purifying you, refining you like silver or gold. People at the time could see the work of silversmiths in the markets. Removing the impurities in precious metals was no quick task. Heat needed to be applied and intensified. Impurities would rise from the hot metal and be skimmed away. Then the metal cooled slightly. Then the process would begin again: heat turned up, more impurities skimmed. Again, and again, and again, until the silver was as pure as it could be.

There are times when we get tired of it all. There have been too many attempts with no results. We're in a rut. Nothing changes. We've failed again. We're ready to join in with the disparagement and cynicism. The prophets all seem to say that no matter how things look on the outside, God is doing something. Somehow, by dealing with our struggles and crises, we will become stronger. The darker things get, the brighter the hope. The Lord will suddenly come to the temple.

I had a friend who opened a restaurant. It's a tough thing to do in any economic climate. She had studied and become a chef. The first year was hard. So much time had to be put into administrative work. She had to deal with both expected and unexpected problems. She had to deal with the cruel side of business, learning the hard way who was on her side and who wasn't. Nothing came easy. She questioned again and again why she had even gotten into this. In the end she lost the restaurant. That's an ordinary occurrence. But on another level, it was a test of hope. She lost a business; she didn't lose herself. She kept learning. She kept remembering the creative vision she began with. A failed venture became a step on a bigger journey.

It deepened her understanding of herself and her priorities. It prepared her for new dreams, and the next open door. She kept hoping.

When the time came for their purification according to the law of Moses, they brought him up to Jerusalem to present him to the Lord (as it is written in the law of the Lord, "Every firstborn male shall be designated as holy to the Lord"), and they offered a sacrifice according to what is stated in the law of the Lord, "a pair of turtledoves or two young pigeons."

Now there was a man in Jerusalem whose name was Simeon; this man was righteous and devout, looking forward to the consolation of Israel, and the Holy Spirit rested on him. It had been revealed to him by the Holy Spirit that he would not see death before he had seen the Lord's Messiah. Guided by the Spirit, Simeon came into the temple; and when the parents brought in the child Jesus, to do for him what was customary under the law, Simeon took him in his arms and praised God, saying,

"Master, now you are dismissing your servant in peace,
      according to your word;
   for my eyes have seen your salvation,
      which you have prepared in the presence of all peoples,
      a light for revelation to the Gentiles
         and for glory to your people Israel." . . .

There was also a prophet, Anna the daughter of Phanuel, of the tribe of Asher. She was of a great age, having lived with her husband for seven years after her marriage, then as a widow to the age of eighty-four. She never left the temple but worshiped there with fasting and prayer night and day. At that moment she came, and began to praise God and to speak about the child to all who were looking for the redemption of Jerusalem. (Luke 2:22–32, 36–38)

This was an ordinary day in the temple. A poor couple comes in (the sacrifice they offer is the one prescribed for those who are poor), and bring their child to perform the common ritual of purification. Happens every day. Just another couple, just another child. But Simeon and Anna, because they have cultivated an interior life, a life of attentiveness and awareness, are able to see past the ordinary. They see that God is doing something here. They see what the prophets had foretold: the Lord is coming into his temple. God is working in this way, through these ordinary events, to save us. They call attention to it, and praise God because of it.

If not already, then soon, Christmas lights and decorations will be coming down. Lights will get packed away, trees pitched. Enough with parties for a while; time to clean up. The house will be back to "normal." Work and everyday life will be taking on their ordinary character again. In some churches the liturgical season coming up next is actually called "Ordinary Time."

As we pass through another Christmas season, will it simply be "over"? Will it make any difference? Of course, it's meant to, just as all the other facets of the Christian mystery are meant to. Somehow what God has shown us this year in the celebration of Christ's birth gets added to the mystery of our lives. It is meant to illuminate our lives. It is meant to make an inordinate claim to our memory. It is meant to usher in a season of epiphany, an ongoing manifestation of God at work in our here and now.

We can hope anytime we want. Perhaps at times of distress or fear or boredom we might remember to ask: Where is God in this? What is God doing here? Or when we have to deal with confusion or negativity or discouragement, we can remember that God is purifying us, refining us like silver. And when it all seems too ordinary, too insignificant, we can realize that the Lord has come into his temple.

Five
Encounter

• • • • • • •

Martin Buber, the great Jewish philosopher, is perhaps best known for his book *I and Thou*.[8] It examines the way human beings relate to the world and each other. Most of our relationships could be categorized as "I-It" relationships. We observe others. We analyze our world. We relate to others in terms of their function: the postal worker, the sales rep, the boss, the pastor, and so on. We do not make ourselves fully available to them, nor do we seek to fully understand them. We, in a sense, use them. And we protect ourselves from them.

This is common and useful in many ways. However, there is another kind of relating. In this relating, there is an openness to truly understand the other. Availability and vulnerability are present. Each person is open to giving and receiving their true selves. Real dialogue becomes possible, in which each person can grow and enhance their relationship. Presence, without words, is likewise possible. This is an "I-Thou" relationship. One cannot objectify or define such an encounter. It is a gift. To be open to such an encounter is a gift.

One's relationship to God can follow these patterns as well. Often God is related to in merely an analytical or utilitarian way. But God is the "Eternal Thou." The encounter with God cannot be merely defined. It must be experienced. God invites our openness and availability to such an encounter. The encounter with God may be subtle, but its effects will be seen. According to Buber, I-Thou moments may come through relating with God's creation, with art, or with other people.

> And John testified, "I saw the Spirit descending from heaven like a dove, and it remained on him. I myself did not know him, but the one who sent me to baptize with water said to me, 'He on whom you see the Spirit descend and remain is the one who baptizes with the Holy Spirit.' And I myself have seen and have testified that this is the Son of God."
>
> The next day John again was standing with two of his disciples, and as he watched Jesus walk by, he exclaimed, "Look, here is the Lamb of God!" The two disciples heard him say this, and they followed Jesus. When Jesus turned and saw them following, he said to them, "What are you looking for?" They said to him, "Rabbi" (which translated means Teacher), "where are you staying?" He said to them, "Come and see." They came and saw where he was staying, and they remained with him that day. (John 1:32–39)

Some encounters are so significant that we can only hint at their meaning for us. We turn to poetry or remain silent. The gospel is about encounters. John the Baptist describes his encounter with the Messiah. At first, he says, he didn't recognize him. God's involvement in the encounter brings recognition, and recognition leads to testimony: *"Look, here is the Lamb of God!"*

We point others to the encounter. There will be a question: *"What are you looking for?"* There will be an invitation: *"Come and see."* And there will be a willingness to stay with the relationship, to keep asking questions and searching for answers, to keep bringing the stuff of our life to the relationship in order to discern God's presence in it.

> We declare to you what was from the beginning, what
> we have heard, what we have seen with our eyes,
> what we have looked at and touched with our hands,
> concerning the word of life—this life was revealed, and
> we have seen it and testify to it, and declare to you the
> eternal life that was with the Father and was revealed
> to us—we declare to you what we have seen and heard
> so that you also may have fellowship with us; and truly
> our fellowship is with the Father and with his Son Jesus
> Christ. (1 John 1:1-3)

The weekday liturgies of the Christmas season draw extensively on the first letter of St. John. This epistle begins with an encounter, which becomes recognition, and leads to testimony: *"we declare to you what we have seen and heard."* The testimony leads us back to the experience — what can be "heard" and "seen" and "touched."

This was of great importance to John's community. It spoke
to the incarnational reality of the encounter. They stood against
some groups' notions that to be spiritual meant to escape from
our human limitations—the idea that God must be kept apart
from our messy humanity. They challenged a philosophy that
sought to achieve an elitism and distance from others. These
notions continue to be repackaged and sold in every age. John's
community recognized that this was not the experience of the
kingdom that Jesus spoke of — a kingdom freely offered to all,
a love that embraces us where we are.

> This is the one who came by water and blood, Jesus
> Christ, not with the water only but with the water and
> the blood. And the Spirit is the one that testifies, for the
> Spirit is the truth. There are three that testify: the Spirit
> and the water and the blood, and these three agree.
> (1 John 5:6-8)

There are different ways of understanding these *"three
that testify."* Water and blood are both present at birth, at the
beginning of Christ's involvement in this messy humanity.
Likewise, both were present at the cross, when, after spilling
his last drop of blood, water flowed from Jesus' side — a new
birth into a new life, accomplished by the Spirit. It is the water
of baptism, cleaning and birthing us into that life of grace; it
is the blood we have communion with in the Eucharist, which
nourishes us for a life of discipleship. Again, it is the Spirit who
accomplishes this: the uniting of our lives and all our experiences
to Christ's saving birth and death, the gift of his life for our sake.
It's the Spirit who invites the encounter and its practical effects:

Beloved, let us love one another, because love is from God; everyone who loves is born of God and knows God. Whoever does not love does not know God, for God is love. God's love was revealed among us in this way: God sent his only Son into the world so that we might live through him. In this is love, not that we loved God but that he loved us and sent his Son to be the atoning sacrifice for our sins. Beloved, since God loved us so much, we also ought to love one another. No one has ever seen God; if we love one another, God lives in us, and his love is perfected in us. (1 John 4:7–12)

Encounter. Recognition. Testimony. Encounter.

The testimony is not static. It doesn't invite us into a mere analysis of the text. It does not find its completion in the repetition of sacred words or actions. That's I-It territory. The text, the poetry, the *"Come and see,"* the *"three that testify"* — all are inviting us to an I-Thou moment. We must come without expectations or preconditions, without the need to define or control. We must come not as observers but as participants. We come with openness to the invitation, willing to enter the divine dialogue. We come simply with ourselves, available to the Eternal Thou who takes the lead in this encounter.

Six
"Baptizatus Sum"

· · · · · · ·

The Christmas season ends in different ways for different churches' liturgical calendars. For some, it goes out with a bang on the Feast of Epiphany. For others it continues for forty days till the Feast of the Presentation, commemorating the taking of the infant into the temple. For still others, it is the Feast of the Baptism of the Lord, the Sunday after Epiphany, when suddenly we are with the adult Jesus inaugurating his public ministry. This, too, is an epiphany — a revelation of God's anointing of his Son for his mission.

> I am the LORD, I have called you in righteousness,
>> I have taken you by the hand and kept you;
> I have given you as a covenant to the people,
>> a light to the nations,
>> to open the eyes that are blind,
> to bring out the prisoners from the dungeon,
>> from the prison those who sit in darkness.
> (Isaiah 42:6-7)

I'm told that Martin Luther had a favorite prayer, more like a proclamation. It's said that every morning as soon as he awoke he would start his day by saying, "Baptizatus sum!" This is Latin for "I have been baptized!" Apparently this was enough for him to know he had all he needed to face the challenges and possibilities of the day.

Can we make that same proclamation with as much delight, joy, fervor? Do we own our baptism? Are we faithful to it? Do we search out the day-to-day meaning of that word?

The word itself means "immersion." In what are we immersed? We are part of many things that contribute to our environment. We are immersed in a physical universe that offers us so much beauty, grandeur, and mystery. It fills us with wonder. We are members of a society that has many benefits and accomplishments to share. We are part of a culture, a rich heritage that gives us guidance and welcomes our participation. In so many ways we are part of an environment that says yes—that uplifts and inspires us.

But we are also immersed in environments that can say no in many ways. We are part of an environment that is polluted with the poisons of human sin. We are surrounded by the results of choices and actions that extend from hearts that say no. We build up structures that say no—that tear people apart, that dominate or destroy. The gifts our society offers become things to fight over; our resources become tools for war; the physical universe becomes something to exploit. We are part of an environment that can spread fear and make it harder for people to live out their calling. That fear fuels systems that oppress and burden people.

Desmond Tutu once said that the worst part of being oppressed was being told constantly that you were no good, until you started to believe it. Our own environment can send us subtle messages, and they start sinking in as well. In various ways we can be told we're not good enough, that we can't do anything right, that we don't belong, that we don't matter. Sometimes those messages come in direct and harsh ways from people in our environment; sometimes they come in subtle ways through the power of media, advertising, or social pressures. They tell us we are outsiders unless we buy something we don't have or become something we're not. Gradually, we start living

a no—no to ourselves and others. We lash out toward others
with the same messages that burdened us.

> Then Jesus came from Galilee to John at the Jordan,
> to be baptized by him. John would have prevented
> him, saying, "I need to be baptized by you, and do
> you come to me?" But Jesus answered him, "Let it be
> so now; for it is proper for us in this way to fulfill all
> righteousness." Then he consented. And when Jesus
> had been baptized, just as he came up from the water,
> suddenly the heavens were opened to him and he saw
> the Spirit of God descending like a dove and alighting
> on him. And a voice from heaven said, "This is my Son,
> the Beloved, with whom I am well pleased."
> (Matthew 3:13–17)

The Season

So he comes to the river Jordan, and walks into the water. He
immerses himself in our world. All of it—in the beauty and the
richness; in the despair, the oppression, the fear. He comes to
share it all. He immerses himself and says yes.

> You know the message he sent to the people of Israel,
> preaching peace by Jesus Christ—he is Lord of all.
> That message spread throughout Judea, beginning in
> Galilee after the baptism that John announced: how
> God anointed Jesus of Nazareth with the Holy Spirit
> and with power; how he went about doing good and
> healing all who were oppressed by the devil, for God
> was with him. (Acts 10:36–38)

He comes out of the water and the Spirit is revealed, anointing him, as Isaiah says, to bring out of the dungeon those who are confined, those who live in darkness. He is anointed, as Peter says, to do good and heal. He emerges to baptize, to immerse others in the Holy Spirit.

It is this Spirit who embraces us and frees us to say yes with him. In the face of the poison of sin, the burdens, oppressive messages and fears that keep us from living, we can proclaim: *Baptizatus sum!* I have been baptized! We will not believe the false messages. We know that we are children of God. The sky opens for each one of us. It opens for you, and a voice breaks through: "You are my beloved son," "You are my beloved daughter." God has chosen us and made us his children, has loved us with an everlasting love that casts out all fear. We've been given a gift that cannot be taken away.

In the face of alienation, rejection, anything that tries to tear us apart, or keep us isolated, or convince us that we are an outsider, we say: *Baptizatus sum!* I have been baptized! I belong, because God has invited me here. God has welcomed me into his people. I am a member of the body of Christ, a chosen race, a royal priesthood, a communion of saints. We are a family, and Jesus is my brother. His truth enables me to build bonds of friendship and community as I step out in vulnerability and authenticity, loving myself as I reach out in love to others.

In the face of the forces that keep people feeling powerless, without purpose or direction in their lives, and the messages that say nothing we are or can do matters, we say: *Baptizatus sum!* I have been baptized! My life has meaning. It has divine purpose. I have been given a mission, a call to holiness and wholeness. Whatever we do in the Spirit, from the greatest to the smallest gesture—even a handshake, a smile, an invitation, a prayer—is charged with meaning. It reverberates in the heavens and sends shock waves through our environment. They are all ways of saying yes to God.

Baptizatus sum! Now we never have to despair. Even when the situation is bleakest, when evil seems to be mounting, we will see the possibilities of peace and healing. The inner peace God gives us will move outward to meet suffering with hope, evil with good. It will engage those who feel burdened by the damaging messages they've received. It will point the way to peace for those who are searching for meaning and love.

Baptizatus sum! We need to choose it, own it, and search out its day-to-day meaning. Every day we can renew our baptism: our acceptance of Christ, our membership in his church, our yes to God, to life, to love. Every day we can discover what it means to join our yes to his, and to send shock waves into our world.

Seven

One Mystery

* * * * * * *

Even though St. Matthew doesn't mention the number or names of the Magi, we always think of the three "wise men" who came to Bethlehem. That's because of the number of gifts they bring—a detail that has influenced the artistic expressions we are most familiar with.

For a change, let's imagine something different. I thought of three stories of wise women, and these stories run from the ridiculous to the sublime.

The first is the old joke you've probably heard: What would've happened if instead of three wise men, three wise women had shown up in Bethlehem? Answer: They would've asked directions, arrived on time to help deliver the baby, cleaned the stable, made a casserole, and brought practical gifts. (Some say they would've brought disposable diapers — that's what the new parents really needed.)

So we know that one. But there's another story that goes much deeper. It comes from a children's book called *Three Wise Women*.[9] Author Mary Hoffman tells a different story about three women who also followed the star and came to the manger. Their story didn't get top billing, though, because their gifts weren't as flashy. Their gifts were simple but came from the heart and inspired Jesus throughout his ministry.

The first brings a loaf of freshly baked bread as her gift. Jesus never forgets that and so teaches the joy of sharing our bread.

The second woman tells a story to the Christ child. Her gift is storytelling. Just like her, Jesus grows up to tell wonderful stories and parables about God's kingdom that drew people into a deeper relationship with God.

The third woman offers a kiss as her gift. And Jesus ends up teaching that the greatest gift is love.

The first story is just a joke; the second story is an imaginative tale that points us to Jesus' own qualities.

But there is another set of wise women who aren't "made up." Their story is sublime because it comes from the Gospel itself.

At the beginning of Matthew's Gospel, we have the story of the Magi, who search the heavens and follow a star. Their journey finally brings them to Jesus, and they offer their gifts to him. It's a deeply theological story with theological gifts. Gold, a gift for royalty, recognizes the kingly status of this child.

Frankincense, the priestly gift, perceives Christ as the source of true worship of God. Myrrh, a precious ointment, used for the anointing of a body for burial, foretells the gift of sacrifice.

> And having been warned in a dream not to return to
> Herod, they left for their own country by another road.
> (Matthew 2:12)

That's at the beginning. At the end of the Gospel, we have another journey—of three women. Unlike the Magi, we know their names.

> When the sabbath was over, Mary Magdalene, and
> Mary the mother of James, and Salome bought spices,
> so that they might go and anoint him. And very early on
> the first day of the week, when the sun had risen, they
> went to the tomb. (Mark 16:1–2)

As the Gospel of Mark tells us, three women also watch the heavens. They watch for another star. They watch for the rising of the sun, to know when the Sabbath is over, so that they can go to Jesus' tomb. They bring spices, incense and myrrh, the myrrh for Jesus' burial. And like the Magi, they are surprised by what they find. They find the unexpected. They encounter news of the risen Christ. And like the Magi, they don't go back the same way. When you meet the Lord, everything changes. You set out in a new direction.

> Arise, shine; for your light has come,
>   and the glory of the LORD has risen upon you.
> For darkness shall cover the earth,
>   and thick darkness the peoples;

but the LORD will arise upon you,
    and his glory will appear over you.
Nations shall come to your light,
    and kings to the brightness of your dawn.
(Isaiah 60:1-3)

A grandmother told me that she came to church on Christmas one year with her little grandson. He was very small, just starting to learn the stories of our faith. She was showing him the manger scene in the church. He was fascinated by all the figures. He looked down into the crib and saw the baby, then looked up at the crucifix over the altar. He asked, "Is that the same person?" Grandma said, "Yes, the same one." Then the boy asked, "How did he get from here to there?" She answered, "That's what you'll learn soon."

That's what we all learn throughout our lives: that it's all one mystery. And at Christmas we celebrate the whole story: beginning, middle, and end. Through the incarnation, God embraces us all in our humanity. And through the Lord's life, death, and resurrection, God raises us up to a new life.

No matter where we are in our lives, wise men and women alike, it is that star that rises for us, that sun that dawns for us. It guides us through every stage. It leads us to offer the gifts of our lives: not material gifts but our life itself, all we are. We give our lives to serve one another as Jesus served us. And in that encounter with the Lord, we're the ones who receive the greatest gift.

Notes

• • • • • • •

1. Albert Schweitzer, *Reverence for Life* (New York: Harper & Row, 1969), 77–81.
2. Parker Palmer, *Let Your Life Speak: Listening for the Voice of Vocation* (San Francisco: Jossey-Bass, 1999).
3. Romano Guardini, *Meditations on the Christ: Model of All Holiness* (Bedford: Sophia Institute Press, 2014), 37–44.
4. Thomas Merton, *The Sign of Jonas* (New York, Harcourt Books, 1953), 182
5. Og Mandino, *The Greatest Salesman in the World* (New York: Bantam, 1983).
6. Richard Rohr, *Everything Belongs: The Gift of Contemplative Prayer* (New York: Crossroad, 2003).
7. John L. May, *Image and Likeness: Religious Visions in American Film Classics* (Mahwah: Paulist Press, 1991).
8. Martin Buber, *I and Thou* (New York: Scribner Classics, 2000).
9. Mary Hoffman, *Three Wise Women* (New York: Dial, 1999).

About Paraclete Press

. . . .

WHO WE ARE

Paraclete Press is a publisher of books, recordings, and DVDs on Christian spirituality. Our publishing represents a full expression of Christian belief and practice—from Catholic to Evangelical, from Protestant to Orthodox.

We are the publishing arm of the Community of Jesus, an ecumenical monastic community in the Benedictine tradition. As such, we are uniquely positioned in the marketplace without connection to a large corporation and with informal relationships to many branches and denominations of faith.

WHAT WE ARE DOING

Paraclete Press Books

Paraclete publishes books that show the richness and depth of what it means to be Christian. Although Benedictine spirituality is at the heart of all that we do, we publish books that reflect the Christian experience across many cultures, time periods, and houses of worship. We publish books that nourish the vibrant life of the church and its people.

We have several different series, including the best-selling Paraclete Essentials and Paraclete Giants series of classic texts in contemporary English; Voices from the Monastery—men and women monastics writing about living a spiritual life today; award-winning poetry; best-selling gift books for children on the occasions of baptism and first communion; and the Active Prayer Series that brings creativity and liveliness to any life of prayer.

Mount Tabor Books

Paraclete's newest series, Mount Tabor Books, focuses on liturgical worship, art and art history, ecumenism, and the first millennium church, and was created in conjunction with the Mount Tabor Ecumenical Centre for Art and Spirituality in Barga, Italy.

Paraclete Recordings

From Gregorian chant to contemporary American choral works, our recordings celebrate the best of sacred choral music composed through the centuries that create a space for heaven and earth to intersect. Paraclete Recordings is the record label representing the internationally acclaimed choir Gloriæ Dei Cantores, praised for their "rapt and fathomless spiritual intensity" by American Record Guide; the Gloriæ Dei Cantores Schola, specializing in the study and performance of Gregorian chant; and the other instrumental artists of the Gloriæ Dei Artes Foundation.

Paraclete Press is also privileged to be the exclusive North American distributor of the recordings of the Monastic Choir of St. Peter's Abbey in Solesmes, France, long considered to be a leading authority on Gregorian chant.

Paraclete Video

Our DVDs offer spiritual help, healing, and biblical guidance for a broad range of life issues including grief and loss, marriage, forgiveness, facing death, bullying, addictions, Alzheimer's, and spiritual formation.

Learn more about us
at our website:
www.paracletepress.com or
phone us toll-free at 1.800.451.5006

SCAN
TO
READ
MORE

You may also be interseted in . . .

• • • • • • •

Light upon Light
A Literary Guide to Prayer for Advent, Christmas, and Epiphany
Sarah Arthur

ISBN: 978-1-61261-419-9
$18.99, French flap paperback

This collection of daily and weekly readings goes through the liturgical seasons of winter—including Advent, Christmas and Epiphany. New voices such as Amit Majmudar and Scott Cairns are paired with well-loved classics by Dickens, Andersen, and Eliot.

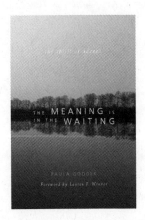

The Meaning is in the Waiting
The Spirit of Advent
Paula Gooder

ISBN: 978-1-55725-662-1
$15.99, Paperback

Waiting is the primary lesson of Advent. In the company of the biblical characters with whom the candles on the Advent wreath are traditionally associated, she helps us to discover very different kinds of waiting.